P9-DBN-781

Beyond Identity Politics

Beyond Identity Politics

Emerging Social Justice Movements in Communities of Color

Edited by John Anner

South End Press

Boston, MA

Cover design by Wen-ti Tsen
Text design and production by South End Press collective
Printed in the U.S.A.

Library of Congress Cataloging-in-Publication Data

Beyond identity politics: emerging social justice movements in communities of color / edited by John Anner.
p. cm.
Includes bibliographical references and index.
ISBN 0-89608-534-1. -- ISBN 0-89608-533-3 (pbk.)
1. Minorities--United States--Political activity--History--20th century. 2. United States--Politics and government--1989- 3. Social Movements--United States--History--20th century. 4. Social justice--History--20th century. I. Anner, John.
E184.A1B48 1996
303.48'4--dc20 95-48468
CIP

South End Press, 116 Saint Botolph Street, Boston, MA 02115
02 01 00 99 98 97 96 1 2 3 4 5 6 7 8 9

Contents

Author's Note

I am indebted to South End Press for the opportunity to present the kinds of grassroots struggles we cover in *Third Force* in a more detailed and substantive format, and I am deeply grateful to my many families for their love and support. I dedicate this book to my brother Mark, whose unbelievable courage and bone-deep politics have inspired me for many years.

Foreword

By Clarence Lusane

Victories! More than anything, *Beyond Identity Politics: Emerging Social Justice Movements in Communities of Color* is about victories won by communities of color, victories that come from commitment, determination, and faith in the ability of ordinary people to fight for fairness and justice. *Beyond Identity Politics* proves that what is needed is not so much charismatic leaders as ordinary people rising to meet the extraordinary challenges of their time. From Oakland, California to Providence, Rhode Island, the stories in this much-needed book revel in the ability of organizers and activists to find the strategic weak points and leverage the necessary resources to overcome the powerful and influential.

Identity is one of these resources, or rather, the sense of solidarity and connection identity can foster. However, identity politics, whether in the guise of nationalism, feminism, or some other form of political expression, is on the defensive these days. Identity politics has been increasingly criticized by activists, intellectuals, and policy-makers as narrow and ineffective in addressing the needs of those groups that have been marginalized by the rest of society. Whether it is African Americans, Latinos, Native Americans, women, or gays and lesbians, it has been maintained that only by getting over those socially-constructed identities (and finding some new, more inclusive identity) can these communities move forward.

Many activists and pundits forget, however, that identity politics is as often a matter of necessity as it is a matter of choice. Some activists have the luxury of choosing their battles or picking their next campaign. But for many of the activists whose voices ring out in this book, their choice was to struggle or perish. In that context, identity politics evolves as part of the arsenal of weapons required to sustain the struggle and fight back through its many twists and turns, advances and setbacks, victories and (hopefully temporary) defeats. For activists of color in particular, the fight is often waged on several fronts at once.

We live in a society that is often deeply racist, sexist, and homophobic, and the policies and attitudes that dehumanize and wound must be attacked and defeated. At the same time, an internal fight must be waged inside progressive social change organizations against views and behaviors that serve to perpetuate skin and gender privilege. The movement for social change, as many activists of color are forced to endlessly point out, is not exempt from the requirement that it practice what it preaches. Thus the continuing expression of identity politics and various forms of nationalism do not simply grow out of abstract theories. It is the continual perpetuation and practice of discrimination and violence that drives and reinforces identity politics.

But as this book's editor argues, identity is rapidly leading into a political blind alley. Despite the ongoing and well-documented institutional and individual manifestations of racism against people of color, "racial discrimination" has lately been reconfigured and transformed to mean the effects of affirmative action on white men! Academic charlatans now argue that we have seen "the end of racism," that a color-blind society has magically appeared in the last ten years or so. These bogus and hypocritical arguments are then used to justify virtually any kind of institutional racism (which is apparently okay as long as nobody uses any racial slurs). This reconstruction of the racial paradigm, far from resolving America's great dilemma, has in fact exacerbated the nation's racial cleavage. It has also put identity politics on the defensive, because for the most part identity movements lack a political program beyond better treatment for their particular constituents.

From the Reagan 1980s to the Gingrich 1990s, the quality of life in America has deteriorated rapidly for millions, particularly for people of color. Regressive and reactionary public policy and unchecked, deregulated corporate power have combined to attack the hard-won gains made by the struggles of communities of color for civil rights, workers' rights, and human rights. The well-known statistics tell only part of the story. The disproportionate number of youth of color who are linked to the criminal justice system, the disproportionate lack of access to decent housing, and inadequate or non-existent health care are only a few of the issues that have bonded these communities together.

The successful social justice organizing described in this book did not let itself get boxed into limited nationalist and peripheral politics. For the organizers and activists in *Beyond Identity Politics* who took their struggle to higher ground, moving past identity politics was not just a simple exercise that required little forethought or hard work. These grassroots activists by necessity went *Beyond Identity Politics*. They recognized in the heat of practice and struggle that common ground can be found among and between communities of color as well as between communities of color and white communities. It has often been the historic task of African Americans, Latinos, Asian Americans, and Native Americans to find the binding issues and concerns by which to forge multiracial, multi-class, multi-gender, and multi-national coalitions. At the center of all of America's real struggles for democracy has been the issue of race and, more often than not, it has been the nation's racial minorities who have made the links and clarified the connections between progress for all and racial justice.

John Anner's brilliant insight in putting this work together not only challenges our notions of the invincible power of the right, but also presents a challenge to progressive journalists, scholars, and activists, in the words of the insightful African revolutionary leader Amilcar Cabral, "to return to the source." That source is the daily reservoir of resistance displayed by people at the community level — people who exhibit contradictions of all types, but nevertheless are willing to put it all on the line for the sake of justice.

While much of the media and national political leadership has focused on the meteoric rise of Newt Gingrich and his Republican drones, the stories that unfold in this volume are infinitely more human and inspiring. Too many progressive journalists have allowed themselves to be drowned by the conservative public relations operations and adopted assumptions of left and progressive impotence in the face of reactionary corporate and political power.

Yet the rise of the Republican polity highlights one of the most critical questions being raised by everyday working people and people on the edge: "Who represents our interests?" What many perceive as the political merger of the Democrats and Republicans is underscored by their common embrace of much of the same policy and political agenda. Both parties call for "ending welfare as we know it," "three-strikes-and-you're-out" crime bills, and obscene tax cuts for the rich.

In this context, the interests of everyday working people are being represented by the activists whose struggles are documented in the pages that follow. Circumstances creates heroes, and the racial, class, and gender battles that we find described here have certainly generated more than a few. It has been a significant contribution to our hopes for a more just and fairer world that *Third Force* has been there as a vehicle for discussion, analysis, and clarification. And now, in *Beyond Identity Politics,* a forum has been provided for a more extensive analysis and discourse on the very struggles that are critical to whether this country faces a just, democratic future or whether the reactionaries now running the government continue to dominate.

In the end, *Beyond Identity Politics* (re)teaches us the great lesson of history: that there is always hope because there is always resistance.

Introduction

By John Anner

Not much is being written these days about victorious popular movements in the United States. The current fashion among most left intellectuals is to assume that the combination of an all-conquering capitalist economy with highly organized reactionary movements has doomed social justice organizing, and that all progressives can do anymore is "resist" and "fight back." What this means in practice, of course, is that the best we can hope for in our political work is to prevent things from getting as bad as they otherwise might.

Although we are a hell of a long way from an independent, grassroots, multiracial movement for justice, we are not quite as far as most left observers seem to think. These days, while progressive journalists are fascinated by the organized right, left organizations are virtually ignored. Every right-wing Christian summit meeting includes a few dozen progressive journalists "under cover" trying to find out just what makes these social conservatives so successful. Meanwhile, the gatherings of social justice organizations such as National People's Action, the Labor/Community Strategy Center, ACORN, Grassroots Leadership, the Center for Third World Organizing, and even the AFL-CIO are ignored or written about in terms hardly less condescending than those found in the pages of the *Wall Street Journal*. As a result, the current received wisdom on the left is that "they" are strong, united, motivated, and purposeful while "we" are weak, divided, fragmented, and too busy fighting amongst ourselves to accomplish anything. Hence the endless calls for a vague "unity" or pleas for another vast social movement to rise up, seemingly out of nowhere.

It is true that progressives are suffering from a lack of leaders with national stature and powerful visions. For the most part, the big organizations that once led the way are either defunct or dysfunctional or both, like the Rainbow Coalition. But change starts at the bottom and works its way up; large, established organizations seldom lead social revolutions or model new ways of thinking and acting. The strategies and struggles that will drive future political movements are being incubated in the places where direct experience of oppression and injustice is fresh and raw, among people without political turf to defend who are willing to try new ideas and experiment with new strategies.

This book is based on the premise that a great deal of creative, militant, and successful social justice organizing is going on in communities of color at the grassroots all across the United States. Nowhere near as much as we need, and far too little to counteract the negative social and economic trends afflicting the majority of the U.S. population, but consequential nonetheless. Indeed, as well-known organizer and author Gary Delgado points out, one of the most significant developments in labor and community organizing in the 1990s has been the rapid spread of "independent organizations in communities of color."[1]

These organizations are winning concrete improvements in the lives and working conditions of low-wage workers; building alliances across racial and national boundaries; changing foreign policy; derailing homophobia and sexism; and thwarting some of the most powerful corporations in the country. The fights are often small in scale, but point the way to building a larger movement.

From Interest to Identity

Ever since the 1950s and 1960s fight for civil rights gave way to the 1970s "Black Power" and women's liberation movements, identity has been the driving force behind many U.S. social movements. Excluded from both traditional social institutions and organizations supposedly committed to egalitarian principles, movements for the liberation of women, the disabled, people of color, and gay men and lesbians burst into the political limelight in the 1970s and 1980s, often scoring stunning successes.

Identity—racial or otherwise—is a tricky political category because it depends so much on choices that are shaped by fluid social circumstances. One of the key determinants seems to be to the society-wide level of political mobilization, both intellectual and practical. As individuals are drawn into the struggle, they start to question the ways in which the universal goals being espoused apply to their own situations, and find new ways of thinking about themselves. The trajectory of the past few decades suggests that social justice movements start with broad, universalist goals (freedom, justice, equality) and gradually give birth to more specific struggles, often based on identity (gay rights, women's rights, etc.).

The modern women's movement grew out of the white middle-class New Left and student movements; like other identity movements, it was originally led by women with experience in other social justice struggles and quickly began to draw in women who wanted primarily to organize as women, for women's liberation. Similarly, the separatist notion of Black Power was developed by activists from the Student Non-Violent Coordinating Committee (SNCC). In contrast to earlier civil rights advocates, who wanted to do away with racial consciousness and create an integrated, equal United States, Black Power advocates argued that whites were never going to give up their racism and would respond only to the threat of force. "Power is the only thing respected in this world, and we must get it at any cost," newly-elected SNCC president Stokely Carmichael shouted at a 1966 civil rights rally. African Americans, said Carmichael, must "build a power base so strong that we will bring whites to their knees every time they mess with us."[2]

A similar process was visible in the development of other ethnic identity movements. Author William Wei details the many ways in which Asian Americans have been active in social justice struggles—as workers, litigants, activists, and organizers in both general political struggles and in their own ethnic communities.[3] The civil rights movement, according to Wei, "exposed the pervasive problem of racism in U.S. society" and "members of the various Asian ethnic groups began to think of themselves, and to act politically together, as Asian Americans. Thus was the Asian–American Movement born."

Many gay men and lesbians who took to the streets with the AIDS Coalition to Unleash Power (ACT UP) and Queer Nation had long been active in other struggles; it was widely recognized that a number of the key activists in the Central America solidarity movement, for example, were queer, in this case, mostly lesbian. Inspired by courageous events like the Stonewall Rebellion and blazing along the path forged by people of color and women, gay men and lesbians built a vibrant national movement in the 1980s and 1990s that took on some of the country's most powerful institutions, including the health care and pharmaceutical industries, unions, the military and the courts. In the process, they forced people who cared about social justice to come to terms with their own homophobia, refusing to allow the question of oppression based on sexuality to be subordinated to other concerns.

Along the same lines, disabled activists have forced egalitarian organizations to acknowledge how the lack of physical access impedes large numbers of people from full participation. The disabled rights movement was responsible for one of the few pieces of sweeping progressive national legislation passed since the election of Ronald Reagan—the Americans with Disabilities Act of 1990.

Complicated Identities

As the victories pile up, however, so do the internal contradictions of identity politics. Identity politics, like any other particularist basis for political organizing, has some big built-in problems. Should lesbians organize around their sexuality with gay men, or around their gender with straight women? Does a working-class African–American family have more in common with its white neighbor or with a millionaire Black businessman? The confusion, in some cases, means that the identity interests of a group clash with the same group's other interests. Widespread Black sympathy for conservative Supreme Court nominee Clarence Thomas and working class identification with billionaires who have political aspirations are just two examples in which a given group may act against its own best interests based on superficial similarities.

The premise of identity politics is that all members of the group have more in common than the members have with anyone outside the group, that they are oppressed in the same way, and therefore that they all belong on the same road to justice. This kind of analysis is simple and compelling, and at particular points in time it is absolutely true. African Americans in the South prior to the civil rights movement most certainly were right to use race as an organizing principle above all others. But race is different than gender or sexuality because of the close coincidence of race and class in many times and places. It's still true in most areas of the country that the darker you are, the more likely it is that you are on the bottom of the social and economic ladder, although this is less true than it used to be.

In a political system based in principle on equal opportunity and equality before the law, lack of formal access to the system is a powerful organizing handle. Once those barriers to participation have been dismantled or lowered, however, the strategic problem changes. It becomes harder to sustain the fiction that "we all have the same problem" when some members of the group are clearly doing a lot better than others, and when the political strategies being followed clearly benefit some members of the group more than others. The result in many identity movements is a tendency towards elitism and assimilation in practice, coupled with a feigned dedication to solidarity with all the oppressed. In a sense, the dismantling of formal political barriers unhitched identity and class; identity movements can pretend that their current particularist campaigns will still raise living standards for all members of the group but the evidence is overwhelmingly to the contrary.

Thus much of the original promise of politics based in communities of interest or identity has been diverted into middle-class campaigns for affirmation, assimilation, and "a piece of the pie." In the process, working-class and poor people of color, women, gays and lesbians, and others have been left behind. In some ways, the very victories of the civil rights movement created this new situation; with many of the impediments to individual mobility removed, changing the system as a whole has become even more complex. While American capitalism has made room for increasing numbers of women and people of color in the ranks of the well-to-do and politically powerful, the problems of poverty, segregation, violence, illness, and institutional racism worsen for those trapped at the bottom of an economy that no longer seems to need them.

In this way, the fight for civil rights has been de-linked from the basic struggle to survive, and the question of how to change a deeply racist system has been set aside in an effort to eliminate barriers to individual upward mobility within the system itself. Thus, the political struggle for gay and lesbian organizations pivots around the issue of whether gays and lesbians can serve openly in the military, instead of on the evils of militarism and the deaths of millions in U.S.-led wars. Black organizations fight for equality of opportunity in the FBI; Latino rights groups for inclusion in the Border Patrol and INS.

By the same logic, people-of-color organizations worry incessantly, as they should, about the number of representatives they have in Congress and in other political and administrative bodies. But that goal has been largely disconnected from the basic issues of providing adequate food, shelter, medical care, and education. The result has been a tremendous opening of opportunity for middle- and upper-class women, people of color and other communities of interest while the working class and poor—finding that class trumps race after all—suffer increasing deprivation.

The contours of the resulting political landscape are well known: rising incomes for those lucky enough to be in the top twenty or thirty percent, level incomes for a few in the middle, and declining real incomes for most of the rest of the population. Explicit bigotry, prejudice, racialism, and chauvinism decline in most institutions, while the social programs on which huge numbers of low-income people depend are slashed. In essence, identity politics have redefined racism; it now means the expression of bigotry and intolerance instead of the workings of an economic and social order that systematically denies large parts of the population access to basic needs and decent lives. Likewise, women's organizations seem militant, unified, and defiant when it comes to middle-class issues such as the "glass ceiling" in corporate America and abortion, and yet unable to form a coherent response to the millions of desperately poor women fighting to keep food on the table and shoes on their kids' feet.

The very meanings of racism, sexism, and homophobia change as the economy and the social order are transformed. Racism at its most virulent now shows up in the numbing statistics of millions of young men of color behind bars; in California thirty percent, in Baltimore fifty percent of Black men are under the control of the justice system. It reveals its true nature along the U.S. border with Mexico, where guards armed with the latest in military technology patrol an iron fence, preventing women and men from seeking a better life on the other side. American capitalism no longer has any use for the millions who once would have labored in the factories and mines, no longer has any need for the massive human raw material that built the industrial base of the country; those days are long gone and the new Information Age global economy runs on a different logic. Full employment in life-sustaining jobs is a thing of the past.

The economy as a whole, however, is still unbelievably wealthy, more than capable of meeting every person's needs. The issues that must be faced are those of distribution, of justice, of the right of all people to have enough to live on and develop their creative powers, of changing the whole operating mechanism to work on different criteria.

A reinvigorated social justice Movement with a capital "m" will have to develop mechanisms of reconnecting identity politics with class issues, putting matters of economic justice on the front burner while showing how a racist, sexist power structure—now somewhat more integrated—works to deny most people the basics of a decent life.

But it's not simply a mechanical matter of hitching together class with identity. Identity politics sees individual empowerment as the solution to victimization, but victimhood is not a sufficiently strong base on which to build a social justice movement, and empowerment is not a solution in a capitalist system whose everyday workings crush the many in the interests of the few. We need to shift—"from victim to victor," as Mark Toney puts it in the next chapter—from the politics of identity to an identity as political actors. We have power in our cultures, our sense of solidarity, our love of community, our values, our families, our relationships, and our numbers. What building a social justice movement is all about is nothing less than figuring out how to claim that power and how to exercise it.

Beyond Identity Politics

Who will mount a viable challenge to the depredations of modern capitalism? The answers, I think, will reveal themselves in the course of action on two levels: grassroots community and labor organizing revitalized by identity politics, and a new politics of identity that strives for identification with other communities of interest and especially with the poor and working class. And these are the kinds of struggles presented in the following chapters.

The chapters in this book are based on articles that appeared in *Third Force* from early 1993 through the end of 1995. For the most part, they are not written by professional journalists but by people close to the action, activists and organizers with an often-untapped talent for writing. While the editors of the magazine, of which I am one, maintain high standards of writing, copy editing, and factual verification, the motivating vision is to describe and critically evaluate grassroots organizing. As the magazine's mission statement says, *Third Force* "aims to help communities of color organize, develop leadership, broaden their bases of information and contacts, and build alliances with other communities. The goal is to construct an independent, grassroots, multiracial movement for justice."

We—the staff of the Center for Third World Organizing—started *Third Force* because we felt there was a need to let the world know that the lack of massive social movements and the general despondency among left intellectuals in this country do not mean that regular people have given up struggling for justice and decent lives. It's harder to find out about them, but innovative examples of progressive community/labor/identity action and success abound.

In fact, the tremendous work done over the past few decades by advocates and organizers for every cause imaginable has in many important respects come to maturity in the 1990s. Social movements in this decade are much less sexist then they used to be; women expect and take on leadership roles in a way that was simply not possible twenty years ago, thanks to ongoing feminist activism. Despite the best efforts of the Christian Coalition and its philosophical soulmates in the Nation of Islam, it is no longer unimaginable for your average community organization or labor union to have members, leaders, and staff who are "out" gays and lesbians.

We have learned a great deal about how to handle racism and bigotry within our organizations, and there are many creative and interesting examples both of multiracial organizations and of cross-racial solidarity. For young people especially, respect for individuals regardless of their race, gender, or sexuality comes much more naturally then it did for previous generations of activists. Many grassroots community organizations are also much more aware of the international dynamics of the trends affecting their communities; this is due in part to the powerful solidarity movements built around the liberation struggles in South Africa, El Salvador, and Nicaragua.

The chapters in this book show how the powerful social forces unleashed by identity movements have transformed community and labor organizations alike, in some cases forcing and in others allowing them to reach out to a broader base and find common interests with communities and organizations they might previously have shunned or ignored. A new generation of social justice organizers and organizations is beginning to flower.

Chapter One

Power Concedes Nothing Without a Demand

Building Multiracial Organizations with Direct Action

By Mark Toney

"Even our friends said it couldn't be done. They said that we couldn't start a community group from scratch with no start-up funds, no connections with established local groups, and no big shots on our board. They said that we couldn't bring together Black, Latino, Asian, and white families in low-income neighborhoods to take strong action to confront big shots in their offices—and still get foundation support. Good thing we're so hard of hearing."

—Mattie L. Smith, Co-founder
Direct Action for Rights and Equality, Providence, Rhode Island

In the 1980s, in an inner-city neighborhood on the poor side of Providence, Rhode Island, small children played in the streets, dodging the cars that raced by. Sometimes their parents would look over at the nearby abandoned city playground—overgrown with weeds, taken over by drug dealers, and full of broken equipment—and wonder why the city didn't fix it up. Everyone knew the answer, of course. Providence doesn't pay much attention to poor people—at least, not until they get organized.

In 1987, Direct Action for Rights and Equality, or DARE[1], organized families who lived near the playground to demand that the city of Providence renovate it for the neighborhood's young children. At its high point, a group of 75 parents and children carrying signs (and accompanied by the news media) marched into the private office of the Parks Commissioner. Preschool children chanted, "We want a tot lot, we want a tot lot." In the end, DARE forced the city to clean the playground, install new play equipment, and put in a fence. Eventually, the playground was renamed the "Mattie L. Smith Tot Lot" to honor the leader of DARE's campaign to improve neighborhood conditions in Providence.

DARE went on to replicate this campaign elsewhere in the city, organizing families who lived near abandoned playgrounds or vacant lots to take collective action by confronting city officials, either in their offices or in the "hot seat" at community meetings. Over the ensuing six or seven years, the tot lot campaign persuaded the city to build or renovate ten playgrounds in low-income Providence neighborhoods, as well as clean up over 200 vacant lots.

DARE's reputation and organizing success soon reached the point at which a simple phone call from the DARE office would be sufficient to get the city to clean up a vacant lot or repair a playground—after all, what city official likes to see 40 or 50 people crowding into his or her office unannounced, or wants to attend a community meeting of angry residents on a hot summer night? But DARE continues to organize families to take collective action to make demands of people in power, almost always using confrontational tactics.

DARE continues to use collective direct action as the primary tactic for winning community issues because of its commitment to transforming victims into victors, to forcing a redistribution of decisionmaking power and to building an organizational base of power for low-income Providence families. To DARE, simply having "a seat at the table" or "a voice" is not the same thing as exercising power. "Empowerment" is not something that staff organizers can carry around in their hip pockets to pass out to active members of their organization. The most effective way for a low-income person to become empowered is to see how people in power treat them differently when they are with a group of angry neighbors with clear demands.

According to DARE, a victory achieved by one person making a phone call is a victory for one individual. A victory achieved by 100 people who organize a public hearing and get a solid commitment from a public official is a collective victory. Through collective action, low-income families learn that their most potent weapon is their collective ability to disrupt the normal course of business in a disciplined, organized fashion.

DARE, along with many other effective community organizations, has turned the tactic of confrontation with people in power into a tool for building organization, and thus the power of the community as a whole. More than simply a method of social justice organizing, it is a philosophy that undergirds how DARE builds its multiracial membership and how the group defines itself to the outside world.

The consistent use of confrontation has allowed DARE to articulate a new kind of politics in Providence, one that does not rely on calls for solidarity based on race, gender or sexuality, but instead shows how multiculturalism works in the most practical sense. The character of American society is such that it is hard to build organizations of low-income people by appealing solely to their class interests (although this seems to work very well for the rich). For DARE, the use of direct action—the philosophy of direct confrontation—is the glue that holds people together across the boundaries of race, language, gender, age, and all the rest.

Besides, nothing else wins victories and builds organizations like direct action. As community organizations, labor unions, civil rights groups, workers centers[2], women's organizations, AIDS activists, and every other historically oppressed group has found, direct action can get you what you want. Since its founding in 1986, DARE has used collective action to win improved benefits and working conditions for daycare providers, greater access to bilingual education for immigrant students, the restoration of key human services lost in budget-cutting, a moratorium on winter shut-offs from the utility company, and fresher food at local supermarkets.

More than Guts

Building effective community organizations takes more than sheer determination, raw guts, and blind ambition. Unlike the little engine that could, many communities' best efforts to build lasting local groups to represent their common interests have been thwarted, often by internal conflicts such as racial divisions or disagreements over strategies and tactics, an unwillingness to make long-term organizational investments, weak membership and leadership development, and a lack of internal and external funding. While the past ten years have been especially difficult for emerging organizing projects, some of the groups that beat the odds have not only survived, but thrived, building powerful vehicles for their communities.

The recipe for DARE's success is a little like the stone soup recipe in which everyone puts in a little of something to create a meal for the entire community—a dollop of membership dues, a bunch of organizing campaigns, a helping of leadership development, and a measure of grassroots fundraising, along with a dash of technical assistance, a touch of strategic planning, and a healthy dose of collective vision. But the three key ingredients that are the meat and potatoes of the DARE soup are:

- Building a multiracial organization (primarily of women), reflecting the racial diversity within the local low-income neighborhoods;
- Using confrontation through direct action as the primary form of collective activity to win demands from "targets"[3];
- Developing a comprehensive, though informal, marketing plan to guide everything the organization does.

These three ingredients have been essential during the past ten years, helping DARE grow from a group of five community residents sitting around a kitchen table with little more than a vision into a powerful community organization with experienced leadership, skilled staff, and a diverse membership committed to working and winning improvements in a broad array of neighborhood conditions. Since 1986, DARE has recruited over 800 low-income families in communities of color in Rhode Island to take collective action on issues that affect their everyday lives, increased its annual budget to $300,000, and conducted a successful capital campaign to purchase and renovate a building that serves as headquarters for DARE's organizing activities.

Power Through Diversity

Much of DARE's organizational strength and legitimacy comes from its multiracial composition, achieved through years of cultivating a membership, board, and staff to reflect the racial diversity within low-income families in Providence. When DARE goes to make demands on the city or on local private businesses, the organization can truly claim to represent the community and is immune to attempts to pit one part of the community against another, a tactic at which city administrations are especially adept.

While many organizations in DARE's environment viewed race as essentially a bipolar Black/white issue, DARE leaders wanted to include the large Latino population in Providence, as well as the smaller Southeast Asian population. While DARE started out as a primarily Black organization with significant participation from low-income whites, its 1995 membership was about 55 percent Black, 30 percent Latino, 10 percent white, and 5 percent Asian—and 80 percent women. DARE's board of directors and staff composition closely corresponds to the racial and gender composition of its membership.

Simply wanting to diversify is generally not enough. In Providence, there are a few groups (outside of Latino–specific organizations) that have attempted to increase involvement from Latino communities with limited tactics that required limited resources. For example, a mailing or flyer is translated and printed in Spanish to invite Latino families to a community meeting. Latinos attending such meetings often found that the meetings were conducted in English with no translation or agendas in Spanish. Organizations willing to commit greater resources provided interpreters to welcome the participation of Spanish-speaking people at community meetings.

During DARE's first couple of years, it became clear that translated flyers and interpreters at membership meetings were not doing enough to increase DARE's Spanish-speaking members beyond a small number. Perhaps the most troubling problem was that even with interpreters, most Latino members would listen attentively, but would seldom speak at meetings. At a strategy session to discuss this problem, Latino leaders suggested that DARE develop a membership committee whose explicit goal would be to increase Latino membership in DARE. This committee would develop organizing campaigns around priority issues in the Latino community, conduct all its meetings in Spanish, and elect a representative to the DARE board of directors. Thus Comité Latino was founded.

As a membership committee, Comité Latino conducted monthly meetings and developed its own organizing campaigns to galvanize and recruit local Latino families. To promote multiracial solidarity, Black and Anglo DARE members were encouraged to attend activities organized by Comité Latino, and vice versa. One of the Comité Latino campaigns, the Bilingual Education Campaign, organized the first large conference in Providence at which low-income Latino parents, as opposed to middle-class Latino professionals, developed plans to improve bilingual education and English as a Second Language programs (ESL). Within three years, the campaign forced the school department to initiate bilingual/ESL programs in all college-bound public schools and education programs, increase parents' rights to choose a bilingual, ESL, or mainstream program for their children, and contribute to DARE's publication of the first parent's guide to bilingual/ESL programs in seven languages.

Perhaps the most significant progress occurred in the fall of 1993 with the purchase of multi-channel translating machines that permit simultaneous translations in multiple languages. Using these machines significantly increased the involvement of Spanish-speaking members in general DARE meetings, and also facilitated the participation of members who spoke Hmong or Cambodian. In 1994, DARE Latino leaders held a series of discussions and presented the DARE board with a proposal, which was accepted, to dissolve Comité Latino because it had met its goals of transforming DARE into a multiracial and multilingual organization. By then, over 150 Latino families had become members of DARE, monthly membership meeting attendees were usually one-third Latino, and two Latinos served on the DARE board, in addition to the Comité Latino representative.

The first lesson from DARE's experience is that it takes a considerable investment of financial resources, staff time, and strategic planning to build a multiracial organization. It took DARE five years and over $100,000 to build significant Latino membership and participation. The second is that a comprehensive strategy that incorporates the translation of all printed materials, interpretation at meetings, and the formation of an independent development committee is necessary to overcome cultural, linguistic, and physical barriers to multiracial alliances. Finally, it is critical that a cross-fertilization and exchange take place between the independent language committee and the rest of the organization to avoid the risk that the committee simply spin off and form its own organization. At DARE, leaders kept making it clear that an issue for Latino parents was an issue for all parents, and that all DARE parents needed to show support.

Pressuring the Target

Very few organizations in South Providence use direct action as a strategy to achieve change because of their different theoretical assumptions about how people in power make decisions. Community-based organizations usually ascribe to one of three theories about what motivates people in positions of power to respond to community demands:

- Morality. People in power evaluate policies on the basis of their sense of right and wrong or out of a moral obligation to society. *We will build your playground because kids in low-income neighborhoods should have the same services as kids in high-income neighborhoods.*
- Rationality. People in power evaluate the effectiveness and efficiency of policies to reach stated goals and measure the cost/benefit to society. *We will build your playground because keeping kids off the streets reduces the chances that they will get hit by cars or join gangs.*
- Organizational self-interest. *People in power evaluate policies based on whether they will make their institution look good or bad. We will build your playground because it will eliminate the negative media coverage and disruptive unannounced visits from angry residents.*

These different assumptions about how people in power make decisions influenced the strategic approaches that organizations would advocate in coalition work with DARE. Organizations that assumed that morality guided decisionmaking would approach targets with a friendly attitude, follow an institutional chain of command, and focus on the art of persuasion with appeals to moral character. Organizations that assumed that rationality guided decisionmaking would approach targets with a civil attitude, providing fact sheets, charts, and calculations showing them how much they could save in the long run, if they but invested a little in the short run. DARE would approach targets with a confrontational attitude, believing that the most effective way to affect the behavior of people in power is to make the cost of doing business as usual greater than the cost of doing business the way DARE wants it done.

A key form of DARE's direct action is the accountability session, in which the target is invited to a meeting at a time and place chosen by DARE, and confronted with a list of demands. For example, at one accountability session, each DARE member dumped a piece of trash from abandoned lots near their homes on the table in front of the Director of Public Works. The city responded by cleaning up 75 vacant lots within six weeks.

While the target of an accountability session squirms on the hot seat, DARE members and local reporters wait for the response. Any hedging by the target is met by chants of "yes or no, yes or no!"—quite an exchange and different from the usual ones between low-income people and powerful local politicians, businesspeople, and bureaucrats! DARE was often accused of not being "nice" or "polite," but members figured out pretty quickly that being nice got them nothing when dealing with the representatives of power. While people might not like DARE's militancy, they respected it.

Another example of DARE's direct action is its campaign to force Almacs, the largest supermarket chain in Rhode Island, to upgrade their Elmwood Avenue store. For years, people had complained that the Elmwood Almacs, the only Almacs located in Providence's low-income neighborhoods, was selling rotten meat and produce, was filthy, and treated customers rudely. Involving people in collective actions was extremely effective in pressuring Almacs to make rapid changes to the store.

On July 3, 1992 a DARE press conference drew 40 neighborhood residents and representatives from the news media. At the press conference, DARE put its reputation on the line with a bold public accusation that Almacs was selling spoiled meat. Almacs' initial response was to deny the accusation and counterattack, calling the action a "sucker punch," saying that some of the charges "border on libelous," and that "none of these conditions really exist."[4] Later that same day, after receiving a copy of DARE's press release, the Health Department conducted a surprise inspection of the Elmwood Almacs, and ordered them to throw out 273 items of food due to improper storage and spoilage, including "green meat."[5] Immediately after the press conference, twenty-five DARE members conducted an action at Almacs corporate headquarters in East Providence. The members barged into the office and refused to leave without talking to the president. By demanding to speak to Almacs President/CEO Greg Mays, and by using the traditional tactics of collective disruptive behavior, DARE commanded the attention of Almacs officials, who agreed to attend a DARE community hearing scheduled for July 15.

On July 15, 80 people attended DARE's community hearing on Almacs. For three hours, community residents, small business owners, local elected officials, and others complained about unsanitary conditions at the Elmwood Almacs. By the end of the meeting, Almacs officials agreed to meet eleven of DARE's fourteen original demands.[6] Within four weeks, the roof, floor, lighting, refrigerators, and freezers had been upgraded; the general manager, meat manager, and produce manager were replaced; and multilingual signs were installed throughout the store.

Thus, in less than two weeks, with three well-organized actions, a small community organization transformed the behavior of a corporation with $500 million in annual sales. Almacs made a 180 degree turn from denial and counterattack to actively seeking solutions and cooperating with community organizations to clean up their Elmwood Avenue store.

By the time the campaign was over, Almacs had made far more concessions than DARE had originally asked for—such as conducting major interior and exterior renovations, hiring a new management team, and establishing a consumer advisory committee with DARE representation.[7] DARE received heavy coverage in television, radio, and print media, building the group's reputation as fearless and successful throughout the area, and forty-seven new families joined the organization that summer.

Direct action meets goals and also helps to build community organizations by involving members in leadership roles. New leaders emerge in the heat of confrontation. People get a sense of their own power in numbers, and the organization gains respect from members, targets, and the public. Finally, as members start to exercise power and leadership and see the concrete victories that result, a sense of enthusiasm and pride develops that allows members to transcend petty bigotries and prejudices that so frequently corrode relationships in our society and our organizations.

Strategic Marketing

A great deal of DARE's strength was built by developing a comprehensive strategic marketing plan that guided everything from how organizing campaigns were chosen and how the phone was answered to how relations with private funders and the media were cultivated. A deliberate marketing strategy enabled DARE to become a United Way partner agency, conduct a traditional capital campaign, and receive funding from sources that seldom fund community organizing—such as Masonic organizations, banks, and the news media. DARE did all this while still maintaining a militant reputation.

Developing deliberate marketing strategies among community organizations is virtually unheard of. The lack of coherent marketing strategies leads many community groups to adopt self-destructive behaviors and attitudes, such as the belief that begging for money is the most effective technique for fundraising. Who hasn't heard of an organization that threatens to cut back its services, or even to close down, if you don't immediately send them a check? Many people hold the belief that their organizations should look and act poor to reflect and express solidarity with low-income families who are the membership. Another common attitude among community organizations is that every penny has to be pinched until it screams.

At times money is tight and it simply isn't possible to do things the way you know they should be done. But DARE always took the view that the organization was going to be around for the long haul, that organizers were building a sophisticated, strategic, pro–active, and capable organization.

DARE leaders took a look around the political scene in the late 1980s and did not see any successful political organizations following the organizational internalization of poverty, which seems to guarantee that the group will remain small and ineffectual. DARE leaders asked themselves, How much sense does it really make to spend the time and expense of running to a copy shop several times a day instead of investing in a photocopier? In the long run, is a donated computer that is obsolete and nearly impossible to run really cheaper than paying for a modern computer system that meets your organizational needs? DARE decided to look and act like a dedicated professional organization. For example, DARE developed catchy names for organizing campaigns to communicate an image of innovation. A campaign with a catchy name is remembered and talked about by members, funders, and the media. DARE received much more support for its organizing against illegal dumping in vacant lots when it changed its campaign from Neighborhoods Now to Project GREEN (Grassroots Revival for the Environmental Empowerment of Neighborhoods). When the state proposed to eliminate dental care for disabled adults, DARE asked organizations to join the Bite Back Alliance for Dental Care, the slogan of which was: Bite back—while you still can. Perhaps the most successful name DARE used was for its campaign for multicultural education: Education = Multicultural Core Curriculum ($E=MC^2$).

DARE's standard stationery was printed on heavy cotton bond paper with custom color ink—the kind of stationery that a successful business might use. Flyers advertising meetings were always laser–printed and sharp–looking, and incorporated graphics. Newsletters were typeset, contained photographs, and recognized contributors, as well as members, for their support.

DARE developed a fiscally conservative long-range financial management strategy to communicate an image of fiscal responsibility and stability. Funders were thrilled to find out that DARE ran a budget surplus during every year of its existence—and staff members could feel more secure and focused because they didn't have to worry about being paid. DARE invested heavily in computer equipment and cutting–edge technology such as the translating machines. They also adopted a principle of making all organizational investments in cash (even the DARE building has no mortgage), as opposed to loans or leases, which gave members and funders confidence that the organization would not go out of business due to debt, a fate more than one community organization has suffered.

Strategic marketing can help community organizations expand the universe of people who support and contribute to their work far beyond the rather small world of organizational members and community activists. It is the little things that count. The things that DARE did on a day-to-day basis, such as send "thank you" letters to donors within two days, and tape an answering machine message that said "The folks at DARE, Direct Action for Rights and Equality, are out on the streets organizing for justice," are things that people remember.

The bottom line, however, is always the people and the power. Direct action organizing and a real commitment to building a multiracial membership make DARE unusual and account for its power in Providence. Creatively blending these elements with strategic marketing is the recipe for DARE's overall success and provides an effective model for any social justice organization to follow. Of course, these elements cannot by themselves build successful community organizations. Organizations must also incorporate a membership dues system, organizing campaigns that meet the needs of the community, persistent leadership development, effective grassroots fundraising activities, annual strategic planning sessions, and a commitment to building collective vision. But if we are ever going to get past the endless appeals for cross-racial political solidarity into a national movement for social and economic justice, some combination of direct action, multiracial organizing, and strategic marketing are important first steps.

Chapter Two

Bridging Race, Class and Sexuality for School Reform

By N'Tanya Lee, Don Murphy, Lisa North, and Juliet Ucelli

Like two cars speeding blindly toward a dangerous intersection, race and sexuality collided in the 1992 elections, leaving the wreckage of identity politics strewn all over. The proponents of Colorado's Amendment 2 and Oregon's Proposition 9, both anti-gay initiatives, targeted lesbians and gay men as a weak link in the civil rights coalition. In the Colorado campaign, right-wing organizers piloted an effective populist appeal that pitted "rich gays" seeking "special rights" against "truly disadvantaged" people of color.

This theme struck a chord in many communities of color, especially when tied to a political agenda that focused on working-class and low-income communities' anger toward the sorry condition of their schools and services. In New York City, where whites are the minority and public school students are 80 percent children of color, the Right's anti-gay campaign addressed the rage that many poor parents feel toward a school system that fails to educate their children and still has not removed much of the basic racism in its teaching methods, materials, and tests. The Right blamed then-Chancellor Joseph Fernandez's "liberal social agenda"—which they claimed was manipulated behind the scenes by a gay elite in the school bureaucracy and on the school system's Multicultural Advisory Board—for the school system's failures.

The message hit home. One Caribbean parent stood up at a public meeting and denounced AIDS education efforts, stating bluntly: "Rich white gay men are taking over. Lesbians and gays are going to move forward with their agenda at the expense of people of color." The Right soon found the perfect "wedge" issue in a new curriculum guide proposed for the New York City public schools, called Children of the Rainbow (COR). The guide included a short section on non-traditional families, including those headed by gay and lesbian couples.

This time, however, progressives were not caught unprepared. Led by People About Changing Education (PACE), a multiracial membership organization of parents and educators involved in school reform, a diverse network of gay and lesbian, education-oriented, and community of color-based organizations came together to present an alternative scenario.

The ensuing struggle over the Children of the Rainbow guide is probably the most significant example to date of an organizing campaign that successfully united gay men and lesbians with people of color behind an issue of deep concern to low-income and working-class people—in this case, the quality of the public schools. The fundamental divides of race and class were bridged in the heat of battle, but holding together organizations representing diverse constituencies was more difficult once the fight ended. Many of the more middle-class and gay/lesbian identity-based organizations drifted away once the immediate hazard of right-wing incursion into the public school system subsided. As the New York City public schools sunk ever deeper into crisis after 1994, the inner-city-oriented education reformers were left to struggle on their own.

Nonetheless, say the activists involved in the COR campaign, simply bringing all the different communities together for a common purpose was a major achievement, and one that offers rich lessons in how to apply the energy and sense of connection typical of identity politics to the nuts and bolts of issue-based grassroots campaigns.

Multiculturalism in the Schools

Between 1988 and 1990, New York City was rocked by a series of hate crimes involving young people: the murder of Michael Griffith, a young African American, by whites in Howard Beach; the killing of

Yusuf Hawkins by white youth in Bensonhurst, Brooklyn; the rape and beating of a white female jogger in Central Park involving Black and Latino Youth; and the anti-gay murder in Queens of Julio Rivera. These incidents put the city and the school system on notice that racial antagonism was becoming an issue that could not be ignored. Demographic trends in the public schools added to this perception.

By the end of the 1980s, a suffering public school system was serving mostly poor students of color with a disproportionately white teaching staff.[1] Students enrolled in high school in the 1992-1993 school year were 9.6 percent Asian, 33.6 percent Latino, 39 percent of African descent, and 17.5 percent white. By 1993, 14 percent of all students were immigrants or the children of immigrants, and over 15 percent were classified as having "limited English" proficiency.[2] Meanwhile, 67 percent of teachers were white, as were 73 percent of guidance counselors.

In this context, the New York City Board of Education under Richard Green, the City's first Black chancellor, moved to implement a 1985 resolution mandating multicultural reform. The resolution's goal was to eliminate practices and attitudes that discriminate against students, parents, and school personnel on the basis of "race, color, religion, nationality, gender, age, sexual orientation, or handicaps." Although the inclusion of sexual orientation in this list provoked controversy, the Board kept it in and established the Office of Multicultural Education and a community-based Multicultural Advisory Council. After Chancellor Green's untimely death in 1989, staff work continued, although with less top-level support and community outreach, and teachers were assigned to prepare new teacher's guides and materials.

One product of this effort was the COR guide, a 441-page first-grade teacher's guide. The guide consisted predominantly of background information for teachers and learning activities for students. Despite some opposition, the Lesbian and Gay Teachers Association of the United Federation of Teachers convinced the Multicultural Education Office to adhere to the original resolution and include sexual orientation from the earliest grades. Elisse Weindling, a lesbian first-grade teacher, was commissioned to author a six-page section on "Families," a state- mandated topic for first-grade classes. It explained that families are diverse and can be led by a grandmother, a foster mother, an uncle, two mothers, or two fathers, and informed teachers about anti-gay bias and violence.

By the time the COR guide was ready for review by local school boards in the spring of 1992, Chancellor Fernandez was already embroiled in a conflict with the Catholic Archdiocese (which, by tradition, controls the Brooklyn seat on the Board of Education) and other conservatives around his HIV/AIDS education and condom availability programs. One of his opponents, Mary Cummins, a close ally of the Catholic hierarchy, raised the battle cry against COR by publicly denouncing the guide. In a letter to parents and school board members across the city, she wrote, "We will not accept two people of the same sex in deviant practices as 'family.'"

Cummins, a white Catholic who chairs the all-white Queens School Board 24 in a district that is 70 percent people of color, found a broad array of allies. They included Latino Pentecostal preachers such as Bronx Reverend Ruben Diaz, Catholic churches serving both whites and newly-immigrated Latinos, Christian Right groups such as the Concerned Citizens for Accountability in Education, conservative Muslims, and four of the Board of Education's seven members.

The Right's Big Plan

In churches and rallies, COR opponents represented the guide as an attempt by Manhattan-based gay and lesbian elites to impose their ideas on working-class parents from the outer boroughs by teaching their first graders about sex.

Fliers, videos, and funds from the Christian Coalition began circulating in New York, leading to an immediate reaction from the city's well-organized and militant gay and lesbian organizations. In demonstrations at the Central Board and local community school board hearings, mostly white and middle-class gay and lesbian direct action activists from ACT UP and the Lesbian Avengers pitted themselves against a rainbow of poor, working-class, and middle-class parents, often bussed in from Bronx and Queens churches. The confrontations soon got ugly. As a gay white man noted after a particularly nasty school board meeting, "Black parents were yelling 'white faggots' at ACT UP members, and ACT UP members were yelling back 'Black racists.' It was one of the most depressing things I've ever seen."

At this point, progressive activists from various backgrounds who had not been part of the guide's development began to brainstorm about a new coalition strategy that could bridge some of the divisions of race, class, and sexuality being manipulated by the Right. PACE initiated the discussions, bringing in groups such as the Black AIDS Mobilization, the National Congress of Puerto Rican Rights, Gay Men of African Descent, Black Nation/Queer Nation, and others.

PACE members, who have long histories in the Black, Puerto Rican, and lesbian/gay liberation movements, as well as in community control struggles with the public schools, noted with alarm that some anti-COR protesters were parents of color who had been PACE allies on other education campaigns, such as the inclusion of African–American history into school curricula, smaller class sizes, and more equitable funding.

Through a series of meetings, PACE and its allies, including gay family networks such as the Education Coalition for Lesbian and Gay Youth (ECOLaGY) and the Lesbian/Gay Community Center Kids, Gay Men of African Descent, the Panel of Americans, the Hetrick Martin Institute for Lesbian and Gay Youth, Advocates for Children, the Lesbian/Gay Teachers Association, and anti-bias peer educators from high schools, came up with a working document that agreed:

- The fight to include the lives and realities of lesbian and gay people in multiculturalism cannot be separated from the fight for educational quality and equality for all children—by teaching Black, Latino, Native American, and Asian–American history, ending gender bias, dismantling a special education system that labels over 120,000 children and helps few, lowering class sizes, and equalizing resources among schools.
- The struggle against homophobia and right-wing incursion in the schools must be led by people of color, and especially by parents of public school children.
- To build new alliances, the organizing has to consciously subvert the idea that "gays and lesbians"and "working class/people of color"are mutually exclusive categories, and

to support and highlight the voices of lesbian and gay people of color.

- Support for inclusive multiculturalism must be built from the bottom up, through grassroots dialogues with parents and communities, not just through lobbying or working in the bureaucracy.

Reaching Out to Parents

The Campaign for Inclusive Multicultural Education (CIME), founded on the basis of the above agreement in November 1993, was eventually endorsed by over 500 individuals and organizations. They included clergy, elected officials, Manhattan Board of Education member Luis Reyes, individual parent activists (most parent organizations were too divided internally to take organizational positions), educators, and community leaders. A People of Color Fight the Right Committee within the larger campaign played a leading role in evaluating and revising the overall strategy. It reached out to working-class Latinos, African Americans, and Asian Americans by going door to door to explain the hidden white-supremacist, anti-public school education agenda of the Right.

To begin turning the tide, CIME immediately implemented a media strategy. It highlighted people of color and parents who supported COR, and who addressed the education needs of all of New York City's children. CIME was working against print and television media that preferred to show non-parent COR supporters screaming at parents, and the well-funded, right-wing deployment of anti-COR working-class Latino parents. Nonetheless, campaign members were able to appear on over 100 radio and television shows, explaining why the COR guide benefited all children, and Black and Latino children in particular. Members consistently emphasized polls that showed broad support for multicultural education including lesbian and gay realities and the narrow support for the full Christian Right education agenda.

As part of a strategy to blunt the Right's incursion into the Latino community, CIME members and Latino leaders such as City Council member Guillermo Linares, Richard Perez of the National Congress for Puerto Rican Rights, Board of Education member Dr. Luis Reyes, and Episcopal priest Father Luis Barrios held a meeting with the Spanish–language newspaper *El Diario*. A sympathetic article and editorial in the newspaper resulted.

Neighborhood Dialogues

Campaign members designed fact sheets, in Spanish as well as English, for community outreach. The first of these, "Myths and Facts About Children of the Rainbow," was used by dozens of parent activists to answer frequently-asked questions and to counter the Right's distortions in an accessible way. CIME also provided support to open-minded teachers by sharing lesson plans and teaching strategies, and by pressuring the Board of Education and the United Federation of Teachers to provide professional development and teaching materials.

Grassroots support was developed through dialogues with parents and communities around lesbian and gay inclusion issues. Angelica Rovira, a Puerto Rican lesbian and grandmother, now a school board member, describes how she rang doorbells in housing projects to talk to families about the COR guide.

"I experimented with a lot of approaches. I used to start by asking people if they'd read the Rainbow guide. I don't do that anymore, because it makes people defensive, or they think I'm criticizing their reading ability.

"Now, I start by asking, 'What's the biggest problem for your family?' They might say someone needs a job, an apartment, health care—it's a pretty short list. Then I ask, 'Has it every been a problem for you that a homosexual couple was living in your building?' I don't think I've ever had anyone say yes. 'Have you had any horrible experiences with a homosexual—rape, sexual abuse?' Again, mostly no's. 'Can you think about someone in your family who might be homosexual? Are they weird, did they bring shame on you, or hurt you?' Again, mostly no's.

"Eventually, they ask me 'Are you pro-Rainbow?' Then I reintroduce myself as the mother of a differently-abled (mentally retarded) 34-year–old son who had difficulties in getting a good education. And I tell them I'm a lesbian. I talk about the different needs that different kinds of students and parents have. They see me as this nice Puerto Rican grandmother, just like them, and they're grappling with it. And I keep asking questions, so they'll ask themselves, 'How did I come up with the idea that homosexuals are one of my problems?'

"I don't directly challenge people's beliefs. But I ask them to compare their experiences and feelings to their beliefs and look at the inconsistencies."

Chancellor Out—Elections Coming Up

By late fall of 1993, it was clear that the Christian Coalition planned to build on the anti-COR mobilization and run candidates for the May school board elections—possibly in all 32 school districts. When right-wing forces succeeded in ousting Chancellor Fernandez in February 1994, liberals and progressives across the city began to fear that the attack on the COR guide was actually going to translate into political power for allies of the Christian Right.

At the same time, media exposure of the Christian Right's "stealth strategy"—getting people elected to local school boards by hiding their opposition to critical thinking, bilingual programs, multicultural education, and ultimately to public schooling itself—got people angry. An anti-Right coalition built on that anger, broadening as activists and organizers across the city began making the connection between public schools, inclusive citizenship, and the future of democracy. Progressives who had little or no previous involvement in public school politics ran for community school boards or supported candidates. CIME allied with liberal foundations, gay and lesbian Democratic clubs, political action committees such as Empire State Pride Agenda, and politicians such as City Council member Tom Duane, Manhattan Borough President Ruth Messinger, and Assemblywoman Deborah Glick, and provided the infrastructure that made formal, partisan work possible when school board races actually began.

Groups such as the National Association for the Advancement of Colored People, Community Service Society, and Association of Community Organizations for Reform Now did voter registration and education. Because Fernandez's ouster was seen as a blow to then-Mayor David Dinkins, who is Black, Black activists from traditional religious or culturally conservative sectors, such as Reverend Al Sharpton, spoke out against the Right, although they avoided criticizing the Right's homophobia. PACE helped grassroots groups new to education issues to develop district-specific education reform platforms, and CIME members helped form SchoolPAC, the first progressive education political action committee in the city.

As a result of these efforts, the May elections had the highest voter turnout in 23 years, and dealt a setback to the Right. Right-wing candidates did well in some white and other districts that had voted for conservatives in previous elections. But they didn't take over any additional boards. In Black, Latino, and mixed communities where opposition to the COR guide had surfaced, several slates that emphasized diversity and a strong anti-Right campaign won majorities. Although right-wing candidates managed to unite with a few allies in communities of color, such as Roy Innis of the Congress of Racial Equality, their offensive in Black and Latino communities was curbed.

At the same time, the situation became more complex for pro-COR parents of color. In some racially mixed districts in which school boards were dominated by white progressives, fighting the Right meant putting the struggle to win more people of color representation on the back burner. People of color won fifty percent of school board seats (the same as in the 1989 election), although they constitute eighty percent of public school students.

COR's Legacy

The COR guide was never fully implemented because of all the controversy, and, as with most New York City public school curricular initiatives, because its planning process never included funding for materials, dissemination, or teacher workshops. As one PACE teacher said at the beginning of the COR controversy, "They're fighting about a teacher's guide? I've been teaching in this system for twenty years and I've never seen a teacher's guide!"

Still, overall, CIME was quite successful in its most limited goal of stopping the Right's incursion into the New York City public school boards, but was notably less successful in its larger goal of building a serious force for educational reform in New York. It's natural for coalitions that come together to respond to a crisis to separate into their constituent parts after the crisis has passed. But in CIME, the middle-class parts of the coalition who were able to manage things to their advantage left the lower-income and working-class parts to fend for themselves.

In New York, as in some other cities, the school administration has approved limited plans to set up independently-run schools that remain part of the public school system. Some examples include the Harvey Milk School (for gay and lesbian students), the recently-founded ACORN School for Social Justice, and a network of selective schools (most visibly in the Riverdale section of the city) that essentially functions to siphon off the best and the brightest of the public school students and teachers, leaving the rest in worse shape than before. The unintended but nonetheless horribly unfair result is that parents who are motivated, connected, and know the ropes can nearly always get their kids into a decent public school, while the kids of the poor, recently-arrived, and otherwise shut-out majority have to make do with overcrowded classrooms, antiquated textbooks (if they have any at all), deteriorated buildings, and burnt-out teachers. Voucher programs that allow parents to apply the cost of a public education against tuition at private schools deepen this inequality, and are promoted by the Right.

But while middle-class white parents actively oppose school voucher programs that would severely defund public education, in many cases, working-class and low-income parents of color are in favor of voucher programs, even those pushed by the Right, since nobody else is coming to them with what sounds like a plan to make *their* schools better. At the same time, middle-class parents are generally in favor of plans to decentralize the school system, since they have the resources and organization to set up effective school-based management plans or magnet schools in their neighborhoods.[3]

The feeling among many of the education activists who are involved with the inner-city schools is that the middle-class forces will willingly join in a battle to save public education as a whole from threats from the Right, but that they are basically oblivious to the fact that once that threat has been beaten back, the public schools are still in awful shape in most places. "They got theirs so what do they care?" said one bitter CIME activist.

Other PACE members believe that despite the divides of class, the network could be revitalized and moved in a more positive direction if more resources were available. PACE is an all-volunteer operation with a minuscule budget, 500 members, and a limited capacity for sustained reform campaigns; one self-criticism often heard at PACE meetings is that the group should have paid more attention to building its funding base over the past few years.

Getting Over Invisibility

Throughout the anti-Right COR struggle, many PACE members were aware that the invisibility of lesbian and gay people of color was part of what made the Right's strategy possible. Members of the relatively new organizations of lesbian and gays of color are generally middle- class. With a few exceptions such as Black AIDS Mobilization, now defunct, and Gay Men of African Descent, they remain primarily involved in identity-affirming, social network activities. While some Black gay fathers, predominantly from middle-class backgrounds, were effective spokespeople in the COR struggle, the voices of the thousands of Latina, Black, and Asian–American lesbian mothers were heard all too rarely. For most working-class people with children in public schools, the cost of being a public activist around homophobia is unimaginably high. Another aspect of this silence is that there are no organizations of lesbian and gay educators of color or parents of color. In addition, lesbians and gay men are talked about as if it's only sexuality that defines them. On the other hand, when people of color who are lesbian or gay—Langston Hughes, Audre Lorde, James Baldwin—are described as contributors to their communities and culture, their sexual orientation is usually not mentioned at all.

To counter this reality, PACE members decided to produce educational approaches and materials covering the realities and contributions of lesbian and gay people of color, and to help create spaces and dialogues, in communities of color, that welcome gay and lesbian participation.

In the spring of 1994, PACE co-sponsored a public meeting with over fifty parent activists, school board members, teachers, young people, and education advocates about lesbian/gay issues in public school multiculturalism. The efforts emerging from that meeting included an issue of the PACE newspaper *School Voices* devoted to lesbian and gay youth writings and two important community initiatives: parent-led outreach and support groups for relatives of lesbian, gay, and bisexual youth of color, and community-based spaces for lesbian and gay youth, where youth of color can socialize, organize, and get support services, free of harassment and violence, in their own neighborhoods.

Two key elements of an anti-homophobia agenda tied to people's real needs in the public schools are AIDS education and anti-violence organizing. PACE and other teachers' groups have been actively involved in conducting workshops and seminars on anti-gay violence and prejudice in the public schools based on material collected by the PACE Lesbian and Gay Curricular Project. For example, in 1994 school teacher and PACE member Bert Hunter conducted several staff development workshops using a resource kit called Stonewall 25 (named after the twenty-fifth anniversary of the Stonewall riots in Greenwich Village, which are credited with launching the gay rights movement). He used the workshop to link specific, school-related incidents of anti-gay violence and harassment with general dialogue on gay and lesbian issues and concerns.

These kinds of people-of-color-led initiatives are a vital part of an overall reform program around curriculum issues in the New York City public schools. Curriculum, however, is only part of the struggle. A true dialogue on what it would take to provide every New York City public school student a decent education has yet to emerge. Some organized communities have clearly figured out how to make public education work for them, and these middle-class constituencies can be counted on to defend public education from those who want to destroy it. Will these same forces rally behind a struggle to make New York City public schools work for all children? The experience of the COR struggle suggests that a "united front" around education issues is possible in New York City and elsewhere, but that a strong organization of parents and teachers based in communities of color has to play a leading role.

This chapter is based on "Fighting for Inclusion," which appeared in the July/August 1994 issue of *Third Force*.

Chapter Three

Building Class Solidarity Across Racial Lines

Korean–American Workers in Los Angeles

By Hoon Lee

Some of the most enduring images of the April 1992 uprising in Los Angeles after the Rodney King verdict were the scenes of determined Korean–American store owners standing guard, shotguns in hand, as rioters try to loot and burn Korean-owned stores. That powerful picture encapsulates much of the conventional understanding of race relations in Los Angeles and other American cities: that Asians are hard-working entrepreneurs eager to get ahead, play by the rules, and participate in the American dream while Blacks and Latinos are the sullen underclass, violence-prone and willing to resort to illegal means to get what they want.

But what the cameras didn't show was people like Hwang Ui-Sook, a worker at one of the stores that went up in flames during the civil disturbance. Unlike the merchants who received money to rebuild their stores, Hwang and hundreds of Korean–American displaced workers like him originally received little of the relief aid that flowed into the city following the riots. Instead, after losing their jobs they were denied financial assistance by their employers on the grounds that the money arriving from both local and overseas Korean sources should be "invested" instead of being used for immediate needs. From the workers' point of view, this was nothing more than exploitation and outright thievery.

Tall and lanky, with graying hair testifying to his long years as an immigrant worker, Hwang is the oldest of the Korean immigrant workers who lost their jobs when Los Angeles burned in rage over the King verdict. Unlike most immigrant workers, however, who are generally forced by their circumstances to tolerate whatever injustice employers throw their way, Hwang found a way to direct his anger toward business owners and their merchants' associations, groups that he says pocketed the relief money that was raised to help *all* Koreans who suffered losses in the unrest. Hwang got together with other displaced workers and connected with Korean Immigrant Worker Advocates (KIWA) in a campaign to force the Korean business community to share the relief funds. It took three years and a hard-fought community organizing campaign, but KIWA and the displaced workers finally won their fight in January 1995.

By the end, say many of the displaced workers, there was a more fundamental issue at stake than the relief funds: the hidden status of Korean-American and other Asian-American workers. "The money is no longer the real issue," Hwang said in a 1993 interview, his voice shaking with anger. "We want our dignity as human beings to be respected." Through KIWA's Displaced Workers Campaign, as it came to be called, the workers won back their dignity. They also tore away—at least partially—the "model minority" screen that hides the often difficult conditions experienced by many Asian immigrants. While it is certainly true that Asian entrepreneurs have visibly prospered in many cities—often through business in the same inner-city areas where many residents live in poverty and suffer high rates of drug addiction and crime—most Asian Americans are working class and struggle to make ends meet.

What makes the situation of Asians particularly conflictual in the modern-day urban United States is their role as the "racial middle," stuck in between the people at the bottom of the racial pecking order—African Americans and Latinos in most cases—and the entrenched white community at the top. This is a very general description; the particulars vary enormously from city to city depending on the structure of the economy, demographic patterns, the origin of the local Asian community, and so on. But the Korean immigrant community in particular, drawn mostly from urban middle classes in Korea, has established itself in New York, Los Angeles, Chicago, and a few other places as a successful entrepreneurial class—albeit generally on the very bottom of the economic scale—in inner-city areas.[1]

This has often led to conflict with local residents, who wonder why Korean immigrants seem to have the capital and other resources to open small businesses while native-born African Americans don't. For the most part, this conflict has been described as a clash of cultures, with ensuing miscommunication leading to hostility and sometimes boycotts, as with the Red Apple market in Brooklyn in 1992. It has also led to killings, as when Soon Da Ju fatally shot LaTasha Harlins in a Los Angeles grocery store, apparently believing Harlins was trying to steal some orange juice. Rap star Ice Cube added more fuel to the simmering fire with his song "Black Korea," which urged retaliation against Korean merchants for acts of disrespect.

In the eyes of many members of the Los Angles Black community, Koreans are able to get ahead because they collaborate with the white power structure and exploit the Black community. Tensions had often erupted over particular cases such as the Harlins killing and the subsequent light sentence given to Soon Da Ju, but the 1992 uprising still came as a profound shock to the residents, workers, and merchants of Koreatown, a loosely–bounded area in the northwest quarter of the city. Korean-owned shops were clearly targeted for burning and looting by rioters, who left many Black-owned enterprises untouched. The events of those three days and their aftermath forced many Korean Americans to reevaluate their place in American society. Many of the movers and shakers in the community, who had turned their sights inward and focused on making it in America, began paying new attention to their relative lack of political power and representation in the city and county governments.

On the community level, there were a host of new initiatives designed to promote peace and understanding between Koreans and other communities of color in the country's biggest and most multicultural metropolis. Indeed, these efforts were and continue to be sorely needed. But a number of Korean political activists had decided even before the uprising that efforts to mend strained relations were insufficient and that the hidden side of the Korean success story was that it relied in large part on the exploitation of cheap Korean immigrant labor.[2] Noting the examples of other worker-oriented immigrant organizations such as La Mujer Obrera in El Paso, Texas and Asian Immigrant Worker Advocates in Oakland, California, activists Paul Lee, Danny Park, Roy Hong, and others decided to build a similar organization for Korean workers.

"We don't think that meetings to discuss [mutual] respect mean much," said Hong in a 1995 interview. "This whole issue of a culture clash is really a misrepresentation. Black people and Koreans live side-by-side in many neighborhoods and apartment buildings with no problems. We need to challenge the establishment that benefits from ethnic nationalism. Our goal is to find a common ground for struggle in order to build real relations of solidarity with other communities of color."

The 1992 uprising only increased KIWA's determination to develop an independent workers' organization with a vision of building solidarity on the basis of common class interests across racial lines. Activists and organizers in the Korean–American community say this was a dramatic event; for the first time an organization was articulating a different notion of the role of Korean immigrants and by extension Asian Americans in general.

"We realized that as a minority community, the road toward successful rebuilding lay in the path of Korean–American workers' unity and solidarity with [workers in] other minority communities," says Danny Park, a KIWA case manager and co-founder. "Those of us who wish to see our community progress must actively fight to break the bond between financial and political power presently at work."

The campaign waged by these workers broke new ground in Korean–American politics and cracked the image of Korean Americans as a community of insular shop owners.[3] Although it received surprisingly little attention in the progressive press, the Displaced Workers Campaign is highly significant as one of the only recent examples of class-based political organizing within the confines of an Asian ethnic economy. However, say organizers, the campaign did not meet one of KIWA's primary criteria for campaigns—that they help build a multiracial social justice movement.

Action for Justice

Even before the ashes cooled after three days of burning and pillaging, Koreans all over the world mobilized to help their brothers and sisters in Los Angeles. Several organizations sprang up to channel the money sent to people whose businesses and places of employment had fallen victim to the fires. In May 1992, the Koreatown Emergency Relief Fund Distribution Committee (KERFDC) handed out $500 checks to Korean business owners and workers, as well as to workers from other communities who had been employed by Koreans.

A group that collected even more money than KERFDC—the Korean American Relief Fund (KARF), originally called the Koreatown Emergency Task Force—also made small cash gifts to victims of the unrest. However, KARF distributed $500 checks only to business owners. Workers' requests for help were turned down without an explanation.

Angered by KARF's unfair distribution policy and looking for a way to get what was their due, 49 workers—Hwang Ui-Sook among the—formed the Employee Victims Association (EVA) in July 1992. Although EVA's efforts to publicize the unfair relief practices got nowhere, the fact that the association formed at all was a significant event for a community in which business owners are well organized into commercial organizations while workers remain isolated and unorganized.

According to most observers, the displaced workers' right to an equal share of the relief funds was indisputable. The money had been sent to help victims with everything from grocery bills to mortgage payments. "Like the business owners who lost their livelihoods when their stores were lost, we too lost our means of support," said displaced worker Kyung Ken Lee. "We workers have families to support and rents and bills to pay just like the store owners."

Many businesses were only partially damaged, and some soon reopened, but they all received the same funds even if they were fully insured. For workers who depended on full-time wages, however, there was no such thing as "partial job loss." According to Edward Park, an assistant professor in the Department of Ethnic and Women's Studies at California State University at Pomona who helped design a survey for KIWA, unemployment in the Korean community skyrocketed after the Rodney King riots. Even a year later, only 48 percent of the Korean workers initially contacted by KIWA in the weeks after the unrest were able to find full-time work. Many had lost their phone service and even their apartments.

Another relief organization called the Victims Association (unrelated to the Employee Victims Association) was set up specifically to channel foreign funds received from private and official sources in Korea. The Victims Association drew its staff and leadership from existing business associations, and it quickly showed its priorities by distributing $2,500 relief checks only to business owners.

The Victims Association required potential recipients to show a business registration and a police report documenting their loss. The policy naturally excluded workers, who possessed neither. The Victims Association quickly gave away all its funds and passed the baton to KARF, which provided the same sum to businesses who were unable to get assistance from the Victims Association. Workers and their families, who had been promised financial help, saw these actions as both unfair and illegal. They argued that the give–away amounted to little more than theft: stealing money that should have gone to workers and handing it over to business owners—some of whom were suffering no hardship due to other real estate investments, savings accounts, and accumulated wealth.

Compromise Angers Workers

Although the protest was confined to the Korean community, KARF eventually felt enough pressure to propose a compromise payment of $1,500 to each worker. In a secret meeting, the president and secretary of EVA agreed to the proposal, after being told that KARF had no more funds left to distribute. Workers were furious with the decision, especially when it became clear that KARF had more than enough money to provide each worker with the $2,500 EVA had originally sought—the same amount given to business owners. It was discovered later that KARF was holding on to about $1.7 million in relief funds, and that business owners had plans for the money other than handing it out to workers.

Meanwhile, KARF was making it as difficult as possible for the workers to get even the $1,500 compromise payment. Instead of paying a lump sum to all the workers at the same time, KARF distributed the relief funds in three stages, dragging out the process. They later increased the payment amounts, but only after workers strongly protested.

Throughout the fight, many workers gave up in frustration. "For the several times I called KARF, the response I got was always, 'We will let you know after we make a decision at the next meeting,'" relates displaced worker Mary Ja Kim.

Unable either to meet workers' demands or to effectively pressure KARF, the Employee Victims Association fell apart. Kyung Kuen Lee, who had been vice president of EVA, was angry to see the workers' organization dissolve, but felt powerless to do anything about it. Then by chance he saw a TV news story about KIWA, announcing its relocation and the services it offered. So, after a frustrating year trying to get justice for the displaced workers, Lee came to KIWA in June 1993, just as KIWA was looking for ways to move beyond simply providing advocacy services and start actually organizing Korean workers.

Banking on Ethnicity

Los Angeles County is home to 134,000 Koreans, according to Park's study of the 1990 census. The community's origins are relatively recent: 85 percent were born in Korea. According to Park's study, only 18 percent of the Koreans in Los Angeles actually live in the area known as Koreatown. Despite its name, Koreatown residents are mostly non-Korean—43 percent Latino, 13 percent white, 8 percent African-American and 23 percent Korean and other Asians.

Community activists say that the stereotype of Koreans as being all entrepreneurs meets the needs of both Korean business owners and conservative whites who want to blame the poor for their poverty. "This way they can point to the Koreans and say to the other people, 'Look, the Koreans are making it. Why can't you?,'" says Roy Hong. For the Korean business owners themselves, the appearance of a unified Korean community of bootstrapping immigrants allows them both to bolster their own political and economic legitimacy and also to exploit Korean labor at rates substantially below what they would have to pay other workers. One of the common complaints heard in the African–American communities where there are large numbers of Korean shops is that the Korean businesses refuse to hire local residents. It is well known that small business owners—especially immigrants—prefer to rely on family members and kinship networks for labor. Koreans are no exception.

Immigrant workers lacking English language skills and other job requirements are at the mercy of employers from their own community, who often ignore labor laws such as the minimum wage, health and safety regulations, and breaks. So one reason Korean small business owners don't hire local African Americans is simply that they can pay monolingual Korean speakers a lot less money. KIWA found that over a third of the Korean workers thrown out of work during the Rodney King riots spoke virtually no English, and almost all of them worked for Korean-owned businesses. Hong calls this the "superexploitation of workers in the ethnic economic enclave."

The percentage of the Korean community identified as workers would grow if the large population of individual subcontractors—gardeners, janitors, and painters—was also counted. Twenty percent of Asian/Pacific Islanders in the Los Angeles area live below the poverty line, while the unemployment rate is under 10 percent. "We have lots of working poor," says Hong.

One way Korean business people prey on recent immigrants is through a scam that involves selling janitorial "contracts" that are supposedly businesses. The monolingual Korean immigrant pays a sum of money to the middleman, who turns over the right to clean a particular building. The middleman promises to handle the dealings with the business owner, which of course take place in English, and then turn over the fee to the new owner. Instead, the middleman pockets the money from the building owner and tells the worker that the owner is delaying payment, or is refusing to pay because the work wasn't done right. After a few months of this, the middleman tells the victim, who by now has cleaned the building for free for several months, that the owner isn't happy and will not pay.

Not knowing U.S. labor or civil rights laws, the immigrant scrambles to find a new job, and the middleman advertises in the Korean-language papers for another victim. One of KIWA's main goals originally was to help immigrant workers fight these and other kinds of abuses—for example, that many recent immigrants are paid less than minimum wage.

KIWA's first organizing effort was a solidarity campaign with Local 11 of the Hotel Employees and Restaurant Employees International Union (HERE). Local 11 asked for help after the new Korean owners of the Wilshire Plaza Hotel fired the unionized, mostly Latino staff and started hiring non–union hotel workers. KIWA participated in actions targeting the hotel's management and owners, and assisted in negotiations.

The campaign showed KIWA staff that a worker-oriented organization can build strong bridges with other communities of color. KIWA's staff was instrumental in researching the Korean firm itself, having access to information sources in Korea not available to the union. But as KIWA activist Roy Hong relates the story, before KIWA staff could develop a strategy for engaging in similar campaigns with multiracial constituents, the displaced workers walked in the door.

An Office with a Phone

Displaced worker Kyung Kuen Lee's first response when he walked into the busy KIWA office was surprise. "If we only knew earlier about a place like this, an office with a meeting place and a phone," he said excitedly. In fact, Lee had arrived at the KIWA office just in time—the group was planning for its first Summer Activist Training (SAT) session, scheduled to start at the end of June 1992.

KIWA had hired Helen Kim, an organizer with the Oakland-based Asian Immigrant Women Advocates (AIWA), to teach a group of 15 young Korean–American activists the fundamentals of community organizing.

After a number of meetings with the remaining members of the original displaced workers committee, KIWA organizers and the workers first concentrated on coming up with a petition to show their unity and determination.

The SAT interns formed the backbone of this first phase. The interns worked the phones, calling displaced workers and getting them to officially sign the petition. Some of the original signers had left the area, others (for a variety of reasons) did not want to join the campaign. In the end, the petition contained the signatures of 34 of the original 49 EVA members. It demanded that the workers be compensated and that the remaining relief funds be distributed immediately and equally among all victims. It was sent to each of KARF's 21 board members.

As the campaign progressed, KIWA organizers found that 18 of the 34 workers were still unemployed after losing their jobs after the uprising. Even those who had found new jobs had suffered a downgrade in working conditions and wages. This gave the campaign added urgency.

KARF was also taking heat from the general community, independent of KIWA's efforts. Four days before the introductory meeting for the volunteers involved in KIWA's campaign, Radio Korea held a public forum about the proper use of the relief funds. The radio station revealed that KARF didn't plan to distribute the remaining $1.7 million, but was instead going to use the funds in the community's "long-term interest" by building a community center. The argument seemed to be that $1.7 million, when distributed, would not amount to much for the victims. So rather than see small amounts of precious funds trickle away, according to this reasoning, the Korean community should do something long-lasting with the money.

It was an attractive argument, but it obviously missed the point: the funds were raised for the victims, who still needed help. After speakers on both sides of the issue had made their arguments, a vote was taken. An overwhelming 86 percent favored distributing all the funds to the victims.

The hearing showed conclusively that the community was behind the victims, not KARF. KIWA organizers began to wonder about KARF's intentions. Did KARF's sudden desire to build a community center have something to do with a desire to avoid handing out funds to workers?

When organizers looked into the businesses owned by the KARF directors, they found a disturbing pattern. KIWA had already filed a wage nonpayment complaint against one of the businesses; the president of the board, Ha Ki-Whan, owned a real estate company; and many board members owned a great deal of real estate. KIWA concluded that the KARF board of directors most likely saw opportunities for personal profit in a "community center." Of course, the majority of directors were business owners, and so most were unsympathetic to the workers in the first place.

"Who was KARF created to assist?" wondered displaced worker Jung-Joo Kim, voicing a common feeling in Koreatown. "If anybody in KARF wanted to buy a building, he should do so with money out of his own pocket. Do KARF board members want to enjoy the vanity of permanently inscribing their names on the building they plan to purchase?"

Campaign Phase 2: Taking Action

As expected, KARF made no reply to KIWA's petition from the 34 displaced workers. After the one-week deadline KIWA organizers had given KARF passed, KIWA held a press conference that featured respected community leaders—Reverend Yang Hyun-Seung, respected lawyer Angela Oh, youth advocate Bong-Whan Kim, John Cho of the Koryo Health Clinic, and Roy Hong—alongside the workers. They demanded that KARF give equal treatment to the workers, and that the relief funds be distributed fairly and without further delay to the victims. Newspapers, radio, and television programs all carried the group's message. KIWA sent another letter demanding fair distribution of relief funds, this time signed by the press conference participants and other community leaders, but again received no response from KARF.

KIWA organizers then escalated their tactics, making plans to both rally community sympathy with workers and keep the heat on KARF board members. One tactic was a signature-gathering drive, which allowed the organizers of the Displaced Workers Campaign to keep the issue in the public view and show that the workers had the support of the community. The main signature drives were held on August 14, 1993 in front of California Market and two weeks later in front of Hannam Market, both key locations for swap meets, which are big business in Koreatown. The signature drive easily reached its goal of 1,000 community supporters.

Also in August, the Displaced Workers Campaign got a lucky break when an enterprising reporter from the *Korea Times* found out that KARF board members had used some of the relief funds for restaurants and other personal expenses, one member going to the extreme of using funds to pay his parking tickets.

Attempting to put their own spin on the fund-diversion scandal, KARF held a press conference to announce their side of the story in September 1993. The plan backfired when KIWA director Roy Hong marched into the middle of the press conference and forced KARF board president Ha Ki-Whan to accept the workers' petition and 1,000 signatures from supporters, in front of the assembled reporters. The fund diversion scandal forced Rhee Min Hi and other board members to resign by the end of the month; Ha Ki-Whan finally bowed to public pressure and handed in his resignation in October.

Now under attack from all sides, KARF suggested another compromise: to give $1,500 to any employee victim who had not yet received compensation. But the workers voted not to accept the compromise and vowed to fight on for the same $2,500 given to the business owners. By this time, the money had become less of an issue than the politics of building an organization capable of defending workers' rights. The workers also decided to keep public pressure on KARF by holding frequent protest rallies at KARF's office, conducting boycott rallies at swap meets held by KARF board members, and other actions. These public rallies allowed KIWA to start calling on the alliances it had built with other local social justice organizations in the labor, African-American, Latino, and other communities.

KIWA also pursued a less successful legal strategy. In November 1993, KIWA filed a small-claims lawsuit to recover the $2,500 for each worker. Kyung Sin Park, a second-year student at UCLA's law school and a KIWA organizer, helped make the case for the workers. He argued that KARF's action violated the fund donors' intent of immediate and equal distribution to victims and presented over 1,000 community signatures as support. The judges dismissed the case, however, ruling that such legal arguments belonged in higher courts.

(Some of the displaced workers won a second small-claims case when KARF failed to appear in court.)

Constant rallies, press conferences, and other actions kept the heat on KARF all through 1994. In August, the displaced workers and KIWA staff, along with a number of community supporters, jammed the KARF board of directors meeting and took over the building, vowing to remain until the association agreed to "KARF up the cash." Hounded on all sides and under constant pressure from KIWA, the board finally agreed to negotiate, and in December capitulated entirely, turning over the $31,000 balance in the KARF relief account to KIWA.

It was a sweet victory for the displaced workers and KIWA staff. A KIWA press release announcing the agreement said it was "a message to other workers that through organizing, workers have the power to bring positive and real change to their lives."

Building Solidarity

"We see KIWA as having two goals," says director Roy Hong. "The first is to inject a progressive agenda into the Korean and Asian community, and the second is to build bridges of solidarity with other communities of color based on common interests." KIWA distinguishes between solidarity on an organizational level—turning out for demonstrations called by other community groups, for example, or working in a multiracial coalition—and "real solidarity," achieved by engaging in common struggles through joint grassroots organizing.

To this end, KIWA organizers actively seek organizing campaigns involving multiracial constituencies. For example, in 1995 KIWA got involved in an organizing campaign at the Namkang Restaurant, where Korean Americans were employed mostly in the "front of the house" waiting tables, and Latinos in the "back of the house" cooking and washing dishes. The Koreans had tried to agitate for payment of back wages and more money and had all been fired; the Latinos were still working but were unhappy with their paychecks and working conditions.

KIWA helped facilitate joint meetings between the different staff members. The language barriers, say organizers, were less of a factor than had been anticipated. The more difficult issue was the differing levels of willingness to take action among the two sets of workers. The Latinos, who still had jobs, were in the beginning less willing to risk them than the Korean workers, who had nothing to lose by engaging in a confrontational organizing campaign.

Through a series of meetings facilitated by KIWA, the Namkang workers quickly put together a common set of demands and agreed to a unified fight. Faced with a rebellion by all its workers, the restaurant quickly backed down and agreed to most of their demands.

More ambitious was another campaign of Latino and Korean workers against A1 Janitorial Company. Latino immigrants are often victimized in the same ways as Korean workers, both through the "job-buying" scam described above and through the usual mechanisms of low pay for long hours and no benefits. A1 was a contractor notorious for its exploitation of immigrant workers.

In 1994 and 1995, KIWA organized the workers to pressure A1 to abide by U.S. labor regulations and treat its workers fairly. KIWA won many concessions from the company, but found that the payoff in terms of community education was even greater. For building interracial solidarity in Los Angeles, says Hong, "the A1 campaign was a tremendous step forward." The campaign received excellent press coverage in both the Korean and Latino press, and was even covered in the Mexico City dailies. "That [the favorable coverage] is making it so much easier to do our organizing work in both communities."

Building the same kind of solidarity with the African–American community has been more difficult, however. "The African–American community in Los Angeles is deeply frustrated," says Hong, because of the lack of decent jobs and opportunities for advancement. On a superficial level, these same problems are shared by all low-income people of color in the city, and to a certain degree a sense of solidarity and mutual support can be built through participating in city-wide efforts such as the "Rebuild LA" alternative planning coalition set up in the wake of the King uprising. But KIWA organizers say that to really build strong relations between the Korean and African–American communities, a much more intensive kind of organizing needs to be done, one that builds direct connections between workers in the two communities.

And while the victory over KARF was KIWA's most visible organizing win to date, KIWA organizers are quick to admit that the displaced workers campaign did not build inter-racial solidarity, since it was focused entirely on the Korean–American community. "It got us the first [goal]," says Hong, "of building a progressive political agenda in the Korean community. Now we are working on the second, building real solidarity through multiracial organizing."

This chapter is based on "Displaced and Demanding Justice," which appeared in the September/October 1994 issue of *Third Force.*

Chapter Four

Operation Harriet Tubman

Student Solidarity with Haitian Refugees

By Van Jones

No people in the world have fought for freedom as long and as valiantly as the Haitians. Sometimes — not often enough — they have benefited from strong solidarity from organized communities in other countries.

This chapter investigates a successful solidarity campaign student activists in the United States conducted during the "Haiti crisis." This refers to the three years between Father Jean-Bertrand Aristide's election to the presidency of Haiti and the subsequent coup against him in 1991, to the U.S. invasion of Haiti which re-installed Aristide as president in September 1994.

A number of U.S.-based organizations and individuals played critical roles in defending democracy and human rights in Haiti during that time. Although a mass movement similar to the Central America solidarity movement of the 1980s never materialized, there were a number of important campaigns and victories.[1] As Haitian radio journalist Jean Jean-Pierre has described, mass demonstrations and public protests by Haitians and their allies reversed the U.S policy to designate Haitian immigrants a high-risk population for HIV infection, a designation which subjected them to immigration restrictions and barred them from donating blood.[2] A much-publicized hunger strike by TransAfrica director Randall Robinson and the work of the Congressional Black Caucus forced the Clinton administration's hand in its dealings with Haiti after the 1992 U.S. presidential elections, and the constant pressure by the 80-odd groups organized in the U.S. Haitian diaspora kept the issue alive.

At a time when the prevailing wisdom was that student political activism had retreated into mindless multiculturalism, a network of activists put together a national campaign to force the Clinton administration to shut down a camp for HIV-positive Haitian refugees. United across race, sexuality, and political perspectives, students on thirty different campuses joined in a coordinated, tightly-focused campaign featuring hunger strikes, demonstrations, round-the-clock vigils, guerrilla theater, and direct contact with politicians. In the end, despite only glimmerings of attention from the national media, this student campaign forced President Bill Clinton to close a prison camp that former President George Bush had set up for HIV-positive Haitian refugees, freeing 267.

Of course, students—as a third-year law student at Yale, I was one of them—didn't do it alone. "Operation Harriet Tubman" was a success because it managed to bring together, at least for a time, students, lawyers, community activists, and civil rights organizations. The campaign built on the strong political networks in the Haitian exile community, was carried along by some determined student organizing, and got its moral conviction from the incredible courage shown by the Haitian refugees interned at Guantanamo Bay.

According to Pierre Labousiere, a Haitian-American activist in the San Francisco Bay Area, students "were the most important grass-roots support we got [in the United States] during those times before the invasion."

Student Activism in the 1990s

Despite students' reputation as being either concerned with making money or involved in self-indulgent debates about political correctness, the 1990s were a hot decade for student activism.[3] More students got involved in more sophisticated organizing efforts during the 1990s than at any time since the 1960s, and Operation Harriet Tubman tapped this energy.

Student political organizations working in solidarity with the revolutionary government in Nicaragua and the popular struggle in

El Salvador were present on hundreds of college campuses, often supported by faculty who had been active in the student movement against the Vietnam War. The 1990s also saw the rise of the gay and lesbian rights and visibility movement, with hundreds of campuses supporting active chapters of gay rights groups. Gay and lesbian studies programs were instituted at universities and colleges that had only recently seen the need to add women's studies or multiculturalism to their curricula. National organizations such as the United States Student Association, Save Our Students, the DC Student Coalition Against Racism, the Public Interest Research Group, and others provided student activists with training, consulting, infrastructure, and connections on a larger scale than ever before. Especially with respect to the role of women and gays and lesbians, student organizing in the 1990s was a big step forward from the infamous sexism of some of the 1960s movements.[4]

The 1990s saw a flowering of political consciousness and mobilization among students of color—with kente cloth sprouting up at graduations and Malcolm X hats and United Farm Workers eagles abundant in every student center. But this mobilization was for the most part self-consciously and purposely cut off from white-dominated student activism. Latent white supremacy among white progressives often fueled nationalist responses from students of color, creating cycles of distrust and discontent. Thus, although there was in general a lot more activism, it was not often carried out by students holding hands across the color line.

For example, environmentalism on campus really took off in the first years of the decade in a much more organized way than had previously been the case. The most significant of the campus environmental groups was the Student Environmental Action Coalition (SEAC), with some kind of presence on over 2,000 campuses and an enviable track record of winning on local campus-related environmental issues.[5] The 1990 SEAC convention in Urbana, Illinois attracted 7,600 students. People of color were virtually invisible at the SEAC conventions until years later.

Cross-ethnic political collaboration between communities of color on campus was also lacking. The innumerable student groups that fought for more Third World perspectives in curricula, expanded affirmative action, support for students of color, and so on were most often students of color from particular racial or ethnic groups organizing to win their set of demands.

Examples of transitory multiracial alliances, such as those formed to protest budget cuts in New York and to defend affirmative action in California, were not hard to find. Sustained multicultural organizing campaigns, on the other hand, were much more rare. The student activists working in solidarity with Haiti, however, determined from the outset that we would need more than just one ethnic group protesting the injustice being done to the Haitian refugees in order to end it. We looked to the 1980s Free South Africa movement for lessons on multiracial organizing.

The widespread and vibrant South Africa divestment and anti-apartheid movements linked campus and international issues in a clear and coherent way, and also linked Black students with white students and other students of color to score numerous victories in the mid-1980s.[6] On many campuses, the Free South Africa movement created a model of collaboration between students of different races and between students and other political communities. It was this model that we consciously drew on to develop our campaign.

Stop Those Refugees!

Student activists are motivated by inspirational events and moved by human suffering, and there was plenty of both in Haiti. The election of the "little priest," Jean-Bertrand Aristide, as president in 1991 was the occasion for days of unparalleled mass celebration among the poor and oppressed in Haiti. He received sixty-seven percent of the popular vote. It marked the first time in this century that a leader with strong connections to a grassroots social uprising in Haiti had been allowed to take power. The fact that he was elected at all is a testament to the strength of the movement that anointed him as its leader; despite many prior rebellions and uprisings, harsh repression had always put an end to such aspirations.

But Aristide didn't last long; after seven months in power, he was overthrown in a coup that ushered in another nightmare of repression for the Haitian people and a strange dilemma for the

United States. After the coup sent Aristide into exile in the United States, right-wing thugs in Haiti went on a rampage, torturing and killing Aristide's supporters. Nearly 30,000 Haitian men, women, and children fled their island nation in leaky, home-made boats. Many drowned.

Rather than helping the refugees, as international law dictates, President Bush ordered the U.S. Coast Guard to stop all boats carrying fleeing Haitians. The refugees were taken against their will to Guantanamo Bay, the U.S. naval base in Cuba. There, the Immigration and Naturalization Service (INS) declared that most of them were not really refugees, but "economic migrants." As critic Noam Chomsky writes, with his usual biting sarcasm, "The onset of poverty [in Haiti] can thus be quite precisely dated: to the date of the coup."[7] Having declared the Haitian "boat people" to be looking for jobs rather than fleeing oppression, the United States then forcibly returned 20,000 to Haiti.

For those Haitians whom the INS admitted were legitimately fleeing political repression, Bush had another trick up his sleeve. Rather than letting them seek refuge inside the United States, his immigration officials stuck needles in their arms and tested them for HIV. People trying to settle in the United States are commonly screened for HIV, but INS had never before tested people looking for temporary asylum. Those Haitian refugees who tested positive for HIV were imprisoned behind barbed wire in a vermin-infested "camp" in Guantanamo.

While running for office, Bill Clinton denounced this policy as inhumane and illegal. But after he was elected president, Clinton announced that he planned to keep Haitians out, just as Bush had. Further, he refused to close what had become the world's first prison camp for HIV-positive people, "Camp Bulkeley" at Guantanamo. Clinton planned to let the detainees waste away and possibly die there, hidden from the eyes of the world.

On January 29, 1993, the detainees—having spent a year and a half in captivity—went on a hunger strike. They vowed not to eat again until they were freed, and called on the American people to join them. The news media barely noticed. There were, however, a few students paying attention: young activists from the "slacker generation" ready and willing to take action in solidarity with the Haitian hunger strikers.

A Plan Hatches at Yale

At Yale Law School, a number of students had been working on the refugee crisis for more than a year, through a student-staffed human rights project called the Lowenstein Human Rights Clinic. They had helped file legal challenges to the "forced return" policy as well as to the HIV-positive prison camp. When they found out about their clients' bold actions, they started to spread the word around school: there was going to be a mass suicide at Guantanamo unless Clinton let the refugees in.

A number of students (none of whom had been part of the legal team working on the case) held a series of meetings in response. Within a few days, a plan was hatched to get as many Yale students as possible to join the Haitians in a solidarity fast. To dramatize the situation, they erected a mock "prison camp" in the law school's main foyer, and kept a 24-hour vigil. The plan called for getting students all around the country to do the same thing. We called this campaign "Operation Harriet Tubman," in honor of the courageous former enslaved woman who led thousands of escaped slaves to the north along the "Freedom Railroad."

The original idea was similar to the "rolling strike" used in some labor struggles. The rolling strike is a way to keep the action going without exhausting the participants; it also serves to keep the target guessing as to where the next trouble spot might spring up. The Yale students planned to fast for one week, and then "pass the fast" to another campus. There, a new group of students would take up the fast and stop eating, allowing the previous hunger strikers to eat again, yet keeping the fast itself going. The idea was to keep this "relay" hunger strike rolling from campus to campus until the media attention finally shamed Clinton into freeing the refugees.

The planning team called an emergency campus meeting, at which students on the legal team spoke of the miserable conditions at Guantanamo. All forty students who attended the meeting agreed to join the solidarity fast.

Then they broke down into working groups. Some students bought chicken wire for the mock "death camp," candles for the vigil, and red cloth for arm bands. Others called a rally, faxed press releases, and prepared to look emaciated on national television. The students figured that, with students at the president's alma mater hunger striking over his policies, the national press would come running—and, in the process, break the news blockade on stories about Guantanamo.

Getting Around the News Media

On March 3, 1993, a noon rally kicked off the fast. Hundreds of people attended, but no national news media showed. Days passed. Bellies grew tighter, but only a few local news outlets paid any attention. A new "media mobilization" was called, making every hunger striker a media contact and giving each one a major news outlet to contact personally. Nothing worked; a few stories appeared in local and national papers, but they faded quickly under all the other news. Neither national television nor the influential New York and Washington papers showed any signs of making an issue out of our prison camp. I got my picture in a short *USA Today* story, but that one success didn't do much to generate a national debate over what we saw as a criminal and vicious policy towards the Haitians.

By our fifth day on strike without food, spirits began to sag. The realization that the press didn't care about the Haitians, no matter who was protesting their abuse, gradually sank in. As one student organizer remarked at the time, "If we want the world to know about the injustice on Guantanamo, we are going to have to spread the word ourselves."

Having failed to make the hoped-for news media splash, the original Yale campaign planning team, along with activists on other campuses, made a major shift in strategy. Instead of playing to the news media, the new plan was based on building a coordinated movement on as many campuses as possible.

After numerous informal conversations about how to proceed, it became clear that the Operation Harriet Tubman organizers knew people on campuses all across the country in addition to members of activist organizations, including former classmates, relatives, and acquaintances made at conferences and events. Lists were drawn up, and the Yale organizers put together an information packet and began calling, faxing, and mailing to ask everyone to go on strike to demand the release of the Haitian prisoners.

It was a dicey move. National protest strategies based on moral arguments usually require media cooperation to arouse public outrage and sympathy. By winning broad public support for their cause, organizers can strengthen their hand in making demands. But here was a case in which the national news media flatly refused to cooperate, simply ignoring the kidnapped Haitians and all protests on their behalf.

The new strategy was to go after the Clinton administration with direct pressure from a key constituency. Operation Harriet Tubman organizers figured that if they couldn't get CNN and ABC to make Guantanamo a national issue, they could still turn the death camp into a public relations nightmare in one of Clinton's strongholds: the college campuses.

Young people had been a key part of Clinton's core constituency. As a candidate, he appeared on MTV and "The Arsenio Hall Show" to dramatize his youthful approach. And it worked for him. Young Democrats on campuses across the country mobilized. Generation X- ers turned out in droves to cheer the youthful candidate, who would finally kick out stale, stiff George Bush. What if those same young people started calling the White House by the thousands, saying, "Look, I worked my butt off for Clinton! I'll never work for you guys again, if you don't shut down that death camp!" By generating an avalanche of protests, phone calls, and letters, the strategy would turn up the heat on the Clinton administration, despite the news media blockade.

Passing the Fast

On March 10, 1993, Yale hunger strikers passed the fast to Harvard University, handing over a symbolic tangle of barbed wire. On March 17, Harvard passed the strike to Brown University, which then passed it to the University of Michigan at Ann Arbor on March 24, where nearly 200 students participated. On March 31, Michigan passed off to four schools at once: Columbia University, Pennsylvania State University, Georgetown University, and Howard University.

Then Operation Harriet Tubman launched into high gear with an "April Offensive." That month, students at George Washington University, Catholic University, New York University, the University of Maine, University of California-Berkeley, San Francisco State University, Stanford University, City University of New York graduate school, and about fifteen other campuses erected "Camp Clintons," tied on arm bands, and stopped eating. The estimate at the time was that 3,000 students eventually took part.

It's sometimes said that the progressive movement in this country is less than the sum of its parts; that there are a large number of small groups working on their own issues, unable or unwilling to get together. But Operation Harriet Tubman organizers found that with the right issue, the right tactic, and the right sales pitch—and a lot of hard work—they could get diverse organizations to commit serious resources to a common cause. Chapters of the Black Law Students Association, Amnesty International, and the International Socialist Organization played key roles on campus after campus, as did student queer and AIDS groups.

Leadership was also important. Patty Berne at University of California-Berkeley proved incredibly resourceful, Yale's Monty Ghivan and Lisa Daugaard showed dogged determination through the entire campaign, Brown's Katherine Dwyer was committed and eloquent, and Harvard's Cathy Powell helped hold many factions together. There were literally hundreds of others who came forward to invest their time, energy, and money, often people with few organizational ties.

By May, thousands of U.S. students had taken part, generating tens of thousands of letters, petitions, and phone calls to a bewildered Clinton administration, which couldn't figure out how all these people knew about the camp. The campaign chants—"Let My People Go—Shut Down Guantanamo!," "HIV Is Not A Crime—Why Are Haitians Doing Time!?," and "HIV Is Not A Sin—Close The Camp, Let Them In!"—were heard from coast to coast.

When the semester ended and the rolling hunger strike came to a stop, the Haitians were still stuck on Guantanamo, but the nationwide student activism, in combination with intense pressure from Haitian activist organizations and AIDS groups, had succeeded in turning up the heat on the Clinton administration and the courts. During the hunger strike, law students from the Lowenstein Human Rights Clinic continued to litigate the issue in federal court, along with lawyers from New York's Center For Constitutional Rights and the San Francisco Lawyers' Committee for Civil Rights. On June 8, 1993, a federal judge named Sterling Johnson ordered the HIV camp closed. Although anti-immigrant hysteria was at a fever pitch, Clinton didn't appeal the decision; instead, he complied, brought the refugees to the United States, and shut down the camp.

It's not often that a legal team and a grassroots activist campaign can work together so effectively. But Operation Harriet Tubman and other community campaigns, along with the lawsuit, forced Clinton to make an about-face. Without the court order, Clinton would never have closed the camp. But without the protests, he would never have obeyed the order. The legal strategy and the protest strategy were twin, indispensable keys that together unlocked the prison door for the refugees.

Build the Movement, and They Will Come

From an organizing perspective, the student organizers made some smart moves. First, they initially put forward one simple demand ("Close the Camp; Let them In!") that everyone could understand and that was clearly "winnable." Second, they focused on a clear target: Bill Clinton, who could meet the demand with the stroke of a pen. Third, they were able to motivate a constituency that had hoped for better things from the new Clinton administration and was outraged to learn that he was continuing the racist policies of his predecessor. Fourth, the action component was designed in such a way to make it easy for large numbers of students to participate, and still keep the momentum going week after week.

Finally, the organizers were able to demonstrate how the abuse of the refugees impacted different groups' special interests. We showed queer organizations how Camp Bulkeley might be a first step toward quarantining U.S. AIDS victims. Women's groups were outraged to learn that female refugees were being force-fed Depo-Provera for birth control. Black groups saw racism. Socialist groups saw imperialism. Human rights groups saw clear abuse of international standards for decent treatment.

Before the Yale students and their allies on other campuses launched Operation Harriet Tubman, the conventional wisdom was that in a world of woes, ain't nobody going to bust their ass to free a bunch of HIV-positive Black foreigners. Because of the racism in the white-dominated anti-AIDS movement, and the xenophobia and fear of AIDS in the Black community, nobody was clamoring to have the refugees "let loose" on American shores. But the students took what had been a "wedge" issue—one which divided people on the basis of fear—and turned it on its head to create a "base" issue that brought people together on the basis of empathy and compassion. For perhaps the first time, white queer and straight Black organizers stood arm-in-arm.

And the campaign reproduced that miracle on campus after polarized campus.

It worked because the organizers didn't try to put the cart before the horse by building a coalition before taking action. This was in part dictated by circumstances—there was a real emergency situation—and in part the result of planning.

So, instead of asking for representatives from different groups to come to meetings to "discuss what to do," the organizers publicized "emergency meetings" with an action agenda and immediate things that needed to be done. Announcements were made in classrooms and cafeterias; teach-ins were held that turned into work sessions for painting banners; everything possible was done to fill large numbers of students with an urgent sense of mission.

Lastly, the students did not work in isolation. They collaborated with the refugees' legal team, which constantly updated the planning committees on the refugees' demands and their ever-changing conditions. They allied themselves with Haitian community groups such as the Tenth Department, and national AIDS organizations such as ACT UP, who were also fighting to free the Haitians. And the students were able to stay in contact with Reverend Jesse Jackson and the

Congressional Black Caucus, who were jacking Clinton up over the issue.

Seeing themselves as the student front of a broader national offensive to return Aristide to power and win concrete positive changes in the lives of the Haitian refugees, the campus organizers got up-to-the-hour information from Aristide's network of supporters and distributed it via fax. The organizers also brought students to Haitian community demonstrations in Washington, D.C. and New York City.

The most important lesson, however, was that militancy pays. When the student organizers started out, most progressives still wanted to go easy on the new Democratic president. As a result, they got stiff-armed on "gays in the military," sand-bagged on Lani Guinier, and shafted on NAFTA.

The students took the opposite tack, lighting into Bubba just weeks after he took office, naming "concentration camps" after him, and denouncing his flip-floppy cowardice at every turn. The "April Offensive" was a key factor in forcing Clinton to make his first policy reversal that favored progressive interests.

Unfortunately, though, some of the campaign's strengths were also its weaknesses. The hunger strike was the kind of dramatic gesture that young people could immediately get off on. But it left folks exhausted, feeling embarrassed and let down when their flamboyant act of self-sacrifice produced no immediate results.

Also, the students organized to build a national campaign, not a national coalition or organization, so they left behind no lasting structure. This is unfortunate, since the campaign clearly showed the potential for a multicultural, standing network of students able and willing to fight for social justice.

Possibly, dramatic mobilizations such as Operation Harriet Tubman are the most likely vehicles for motivating students to participate in a broader movement for social justice. Not since the days of the anti-apartheid movement had white and African-American students come together with such common purpose. The added organizational strength and militancy of the queer community and other communities of color, along with women's organizations, gave Operation Harriet Tubman a vibrancy and emotional impact that lasted well beyond the campaign itself.

For me, it was a preview of the type of movement we need to save us all in this country: a broad social movement comprising different communities and independent organizations, cooperating in their own enlightened self-interest. The tricky part is to find the right campaigns, and provide leadership.

This chapter is based on "Operation Harriet Tubman," which appeared in the July/August 1994 issue of *Third Force.*

Chapter Five

How the Empress Gets Her Clothes

Asian Immigrant Women Fight Fashion Designer Jessica McClintock

By Gary Delgado

One of the most enduring sales gimmicks is the promise that "what you see is what you get." The phrase is used in refrains by rappers, TV commercials for hamburger chains try to get us to hum it, and computer programmers use the popular if unpronounceable "wysiwyg" to assure us that what we see on our computer screens will show up on the printer.

The problem with the phrase is that it is fundamentally false. In the mid-1800s, Karl Marx wrote that the real "magic" of capitalism is the fetishism of the commodity—the ability to present any product devoid of its history. What we "get" with each purchase is not simply the piece of goods. The product includes the effects on the earth of harvesting or extracting raw materials, the labor involved in making the goods and the conditions under which they are made, the transport of the product, the structure of the business, the costs of packaging and marketing the product, and the costs of disposing of the product waste. Of course, we don't think about any of these things when we pay our 75 cents for a "you've got the right one baby" Pepsi, $2.49 for a Mickey D's "happy meal," or even $175 for a Jessica McClintock dress. Because of the particular brand of magic embedded in our economic system, we are able to see the hamburger without the cow, and the $175 dress without the fingers that sew it.

The following pages document the efforts of the Asian Immigrant Women Advocates (AIWA) to secure back wages and just treatment for Asian immigrant women working in the garment industry. AIWA was able to redress the grievances of 12 garment workers who never received payment for their work from a clothing contractor in the employ of one of the most successful clothing designers in the country. AIWA's work illustrates equally important lessons in the mobilization of young activists and serves as an example of how a community organization used education, public disruption, media events, and an effective boycott to slash through the sweatshop curtains and make visible the plight of garment workers.

Insufficient Funds

Like most community-based campaigns, this one started with a problem. On a cloudy afternoon in May 1992, a small group of women entered AIWA's office and explained their situation: after working twelve hours a day, seven days a week for the Lucky Sewing Company, they were given $15,000 in paychecks that soon came back from their employer's account marked "insufficient funds."

This was not the first time AIWA had heard these kinds of complaints. Although the major activities of the organization are literacy and leadership development classes for seamstresses, electronics assemblers, hotel maids, and janitors, as well as "know your rights" sessions held in Chinese, Vietnamese, Tagalog, and Korean, AIWA had addressed workers' grievances at a workers' speak-out with representatives of the Wage and Hour Division of the Department of Labor.

AIWA's Chinese organizer, Ken Fong, investigated the finances of Lucky Sewing and found that the company had declared bankruptcy and owed creditors over $350,000. Although under bankruptcy law Lucky workers were first in line for payment, the company had few assets, making back pay for the seamstresses unlikely. The case of Lucky Sewing was not unusual. In July 1991, the owner of nine San Francisco Bay Area sewing shops disappeared, owing 450 seamstresses back wages. When the owner was apprehended seven months later, she was charged with defrauding banks of almost $20 million and defrauding employees of over $1 million in wages.[1]

Discovering that they would have no recourse from the Lucky Sewing Company, AIWA organizers decided to explore with the seamstresses the possibility of seeking compensation for their back wages directly from the clothing manufacturer, even though the manufacturer was not legally liable. Research by AIWA organizers uncovered the fact that Lucky Sewing had been exclusively contracted by one apparel manufacturer for almost ten years. This firm—Jessica McClintock, Inc.—reported a 1991 gross income of $145 million from sales of designer perfume, evening wear, and prom, wedding, and children's' dresses, which were sold in exclusive boutiques and major department stores.

AIWA's director Young Hai Shin recalls, "I knew that the Farm Labor Organizing Committee had organized contractors and farmworkers in the agricultural sector to negotiate with Campbell's [Soup Company], and we had been supportive when contractors had decided to set up a contractors' association. However, I had no idea if the women who'd worked at Lucky Sewing would be willing to challenge a major clothing manufacturer." After a series of discussions with the seamstresses, AIWA's staff and five of the seamstresses visited McClintock's boutique on Sutter Street in San Francisco. One of the seamstresses, who was owed pay for two and a half months of 10-hours-a-day, seven-days-a-week work, declared, "I was angry, I didn't expect our dresses to sell for such a high price."[2] "*That's* clearly what decided them," recalls Shin. "The fact that dresses the women had earned $5 to make were selling in that boutique for $175 gave the women the courage to ask McClintock for back wages."[3]

In the middle and late 1980s, the U.S.-based apparel industry was having a difficult time competing with clothes produced overseas. As a 1991 analysis of the industry published in *Business Week* noted, "Imports are up and profits are way down."[4] Many of the garments sold in the U.S. were, and still are, produced in developing countries where working conditions are not subject to U.S. health and safety standards, labor costs are significantly lower, and unions are nonexistent. Many of the garment shops serving the U.S. market are in China, Taiwan, and Korea. In addition, between 1983 and 1989, 100,000 sewing jobs have been created in Caribbean countries, including Haiti, Costa Rica, the Dominican Republic, and Jamaica.[5] According to Katie Quan of the International Ladies Garment Workers Union in San Francisco, "a (garment) worker in Mexico gets paid $4.50 a day, in Guatemala it's only $2 a day, and in El Salvador, it's less than that."[6]

To retain easy access to the U.S. market and manufacturing costs roughly equivalent to those in developing countries, some U.S. apparel manufacturers have hired "independent" contractors for the production of specific clothing lines. These contractors, who compete to keep costs low, are notorious for poorly lit and inadequately ventilated shops, substandard pay, no overtime or vacation pay, no health or worker's compensation benefits, and the use of underage workers.

There are approximately 20,000 sewing jobs in such sweatshop conditions in the San Francisco area. And, while Department of Labor raids on the shops often produce citations and fines for unpaid worker's compensation, payroll discrepancies, blocked access, and poor ventilation, little has been done to address sweatshop conditions overall. However, the situation is literally "made to order" for clothing manufacturers who are, according to researchers for the Economic Policy Institute, "close to being competitive with some Third World imports."[7]

Aside from the "competitive" price of the clothing, the contractor arrangement sets up an effective (often Asian) buffer between the seamstress and the giants of the apparel industry. Unlike the electronics industry, clothing manufactures aren't responsible for the conditions and occurrences in a contractor's shop. Although bills to crack down on "stitch and ditch" sewing shops have been passed by the California legislature, governors George Deukmejian and Pete Wilson (after heavy lobbying by the Coalition of Apparel Industries) have vetoed the proposed legislation three times.

The Campaign's Beginnings

Community organizers classically launch direct action campaigns with a series of incremental activities in which human, financial, and communication resources are mobilized and focused on a target or series of targets to win specific demands. Good community organizing campaigns deliver concrete benefits to members of the community organization, develop leadership, clearly delineate the "sides" of the issue, and build the power of the organization.[8]

Most campaigns start out as problems encountered by a particular constituency that can be solved by the actions of one or two powerful actors. However, because of Jessica McClintock's personal reputation as both a progressive woman and an active supporter of anti-AIDS work in San Francisco, the seamstresses and AIWA staff workers were hoping to avoid a confrontation and to instead appeal to McClintock's sense of fairness. In the early stages of what was to develop into the Garment Workers Justice Campaign, the aim of the campaign was to urge her to "do the right thing" and pay the garment workers the $15,000 in back wages they were owed by Lucky Sewing.

AIWA began organizing by writing a public letter to Jessica McClintock in September 1992, reminding her of her "on the record" commitment to social responsibility and requesting that she pay the workers their back wages and grant the laid-off workers a two-year independent contract to continue sewing for McClintock Inc. Understanding that the letter was necessary to lay out the garment workers' demands, the group simultaneously organized a public support meeting for the seamstresses that was attended by 150 activists from community, religious, labor, student, and women's organizations.

In a rapid series of events in October 1992, Jessica McClintock denied responsibility for the workers' back wages, a front-page article about the plight of the seamstresses appeared in the *San Francisco Examiner*, and AIWA organized a rally for "Fairness and Solidarity," attended by 250 people, replete with signs bearing Chinese characters calling for "power, fairness, and solidarity." At the rally, one of the seamstresses, wearing a mask to conceal her identity, told the crowd about signs in the sweatshop warning workers against "loud talking and going to the bathroom." Demonstrators chanted "Jessie, Jessie, stitch by stitch, sweatshop labor made you rich."

Refusals by McClintock Inc. to respond to the seamstresses' requests led to the formation of a seamstress-led organizing committee. Its first action was to set up a picket line at McClintock Inc.'s downtown San Francisco store. At a second picket on October 20, the campaign announced a national boycott of McClintock clothes. As picketers, angry with McClintock Inc.'s refusal to meet seamstress demands, chanted, "Your dresses, they're pink; your wages, they stink," young supporters handed out pink and black day-glow leaflets describing the aims of the boycott to passersby.

According to political scientist Michael Lipsky, in order for protest activities to achieve institutional change protest leaders must nurture and sustain an organization; adapt to the mass media; choose tactics that will give the campaign the most favorable exposure possible; develop tactics to affect a "third party" of potential liberal supporters; and influence the target to accede to the group's demands.[9] Over the next sixteen months, AIWA campaign organizers worked to accomplish all these goals. Their plan involved expanding the geographic and constituent base of campaign pressure activities and increasing the visibility of the garment workers, the boycott, and McClintock Inc.'s response to both.

Constituent Expansion

AIWA is a relatively small organization with a staff of seven and an annual budget of $350,000. Campaign organizers knew from the very beginning of their efforts that, in order to make an impact on McClintock, they would need to demonstrate public support for the seamstresses from a wide range of constituents and, in the words of campaign organizer Miriam Louie, "to show them that we could affect their business."[10]

Among the campaign strategists was Alfredo De Avila, Young Shin's spouse, Training Director of the Center for Third World Organizing, and veteran of United Farm Workers and Texas Farmworkers campaigns. De Avila helped the campaign organizers identify potential campaign supporters.

Boycott organizer Helen Kim developed strategies for reaching the different constituencies.[11] Describing the strategy, Kim notes, "We used every connection we had—especially family and friends. We had good connections to the students at UC Berkeley, so we asked them to help us get in touch with other students around the country. When our student contacts in the Midwest ran dry, I contacted my brother who'd just graduated from college and asked him to get his friends involved in the boycott. We began to strategize how AIWA's participation in a number of networks, including the Urban-Rural Mission and the Voluntary Services Network of the United Methodist Church and the Workers Leadership Development Network, could be turned to our advantage in the campaign. We secured additional support from my contacts in the mentoring program I participate in at the Center for Third World Organizing. Young has carried the seamstresses' story into a number of networks of women's organizations and the national response from Asian-American organizations, including the Asian Pacific American Labor Alliance (APALA), has been tremendous."[12]

Working with over 150 local community organizations, AIWA launched pickets in eleven cities and secured campaign endorsements from over 400 church, labor, and community organizations. In part, the key to the campaign's success in developing support from a wide variety of constituent groups was the organizers' willingness to accept offers of support from organizations according to their interests, resources, and abilities. For example, campaign staff was open to the Southwest Network's endorsement and letter writing campaign; the picketing efforts of the Korean Immigrant Workers Association, the United Methodist Voluntary Services program in Los Angeles, Action for a Better Community in Denver, Direct Action for Rights and Equality in Providence, and the Chinese Staff and Workers Association in New York; and the development of a "National Day of Solidarity with Garment Workers" organized by Asian Pacific American students. Local support committees participated in educational presentations, media actions, and pickets of ten McClintock-owned stores, as well as stores that carried McClintock Inc. products.

AIWA's strategy to convince people to participate in the campaign was to suggest small non-threatening tasks, such as mailing postcards that protested the treatment of the seamstresses; then to escalate the activities to local research on the status of garment workers to "give the campaign a local hook"; and finally to build local actions, often including individuals from several organizations and linking with APALA as well as the International Ladies Garment Workers Union.[13] To build a student network, campaign staff worked with a core group of volunteers from four college campuses to conduct outreach on thirty campuses over the summer of 1993. By the beginning of the fall semester, AIWA had support chapters on 22 campuses.

A second tool was direct appeals to a middle-class constituency through an ad campaign. AIWA was assisted in its campaign efforts by the Public Media Center (PMC), the premier public interest advertising agency in the country. Directed by Herb Chao Gunther, himself a Chinese immigrant, PMC's pro bono work on the campaign included development of the ad imagery. From the very first ad—"Let Them Eat Lace"—PMC began the difficult task of making the people behind the sewing machines visible. Placed in the Western edition of the *New York Times*, the ad was a work of contrasts. A simply-dressed older Asian woman held a bright, frilly white dress against a drab background reminiscent of conditions in garment sweatshops in the nineteenth century—sewing machines, thread, no viable ventilation, and stacked boxes. Bold white-on-black type in the center box reads: "It's rags to riches for Jessica McClintock. But the women who sew in the sweatshops have still not been paid. You can help." A second ad in December 1992 titled "Fantasy vs. Reality" continued the theme of contrasts. The copy read "When you see Jessica McClintock's holiday windows this year, think about the reality behind them: sweatshop women facing a cold, grim Christmas."

"The ads," says PMC director Gunther, "had a number of purposes. By putting a human face on the seamstresses, we made their plight more understandable. And, since the industry lobbyists had already had their say in getting [Governor] Wilson to veto a bill which would make manufacturers responsible for the actions of contractors, we were able to take the women's case directly to the public. We were also able to use the ad to contrast the case of one woman who'd become a multimillionaire with other women who'd actually made the products under miserable conditions, but had nothing to show for it."[14]

Building on the interest generated by the ads, AIWA was able to get something that most community-based campaigns never get — fair, frequent, and positive coverage of their side of the story. Assessing the press strategy, Miriam Louie noted that the ads "opened up the press to calling us for follow-up feature stories—especially after Jessica McClintock took out an ad. We were fortunate that the Center for

Investigative Reporting did a story on the seamstresses' struggle which appeared in the *Los Angeles Times Magazine*. A slightly abridged version of the piece appeared in the *San Francisco Chronicle/Examiner's Sunday Magazine*. After that, many of the newspapers began to call us as a source."

When asked about coverage in the ethnic language press, Louie replied, "It is particularly important to have our story appear in the Chinese and Korean-language newspapers, to maintain support in the Asian community. The *Sing Tao* (Cantonese) and *World Journal* (Mandarin), along with *Asian Week*, have covered our events closely, especially in the beginning. It is true, however, that the coverage has changed since McClintock hired Asian PR firms in the Bay Area and Los Angeles last December. Although we still get fairly good coverage, it was in the Chinese-language newspapers that the names of the seamstresses who refused McClintock's deal were printed, and those women have been harassed and blacklisted." AIWA was planning to encourage teenagers to honor the boycott through fashion magazine stories. Asked about the timing of the effort, Louie smiled. "We'd like to see the stories surface just before prom time."[15]

AIWA also used an endorsement strategy to develop support for the campaign. In May 1993, the campaign sponsored community hearings and invited clergy and local and state politicians to attend. As a result of these hearings, the Oakland City Council voted to convene a special task force to investigate industry working conditions. Both the City Council of Berkeley and the Alameda County Board of Supervisors voted to endorse the campaign. In each case a representative of McClintock Inc. unsuccessfully attempted to stop the endorsement.[16] On a parallel track, AIWA was able to parlay the organization's connections to religious organizations into campaign endorsements, letter-writing efforts, and, in two cases, picketing organized by clergy.

Although the campaign was quite effective in mobilizing support from a wide array of individuals and organizations, the most responsive constituency was the Asian community—especially young Asian women. "On a very basic level," explains Helen Kim, the 30-year-old daughter of an electronics worker, "it is their aunts, their cousins, and, for many, their mothers who they're fighting for. These young women are angry about the way their relatives were treated, angry about how these seamstresses are treated, and angry about how they themselves are treated because of this model minority myth. Many young women who developed as leaders in this campaign felt like this was *their* fight, and this campaign offered them an opportunity to channel their anger in a productive manner in an *Asian-American* struggle."[17]

The Empire Strikes Back

After over fifty years of practice, there are few new responses by targets of community campaigns. Besides acceding to a group's demands, the catalogue of responses from institutions on the "other side of the fence" from community groups includes: attempts to discredit the community organization; efforts to co-opt the campaign's leadership, membership, or allies; offering token as opposed to real satisfaction; delaying tactics; legal entanglement; acceding to the wishes of a less radical organization (created or co-opted by the target); publishing misleading information about the "facts" of the situation; and various destabilizing tactics including infiltration, surveillance, physical intimidation, and the theft of valuable information.[18]

McClintock Inc. employed quite a number of these tactics. In an attempt to reduce public support for the campaign by accusing AIWA of being a union in disguise, Bernard Lax, president of the Coalition of Apparel Industries of California, wrote a letter in August 1993 to the *Los Angeles Times*. He described AIWA's efforts to "crucify Jessica McClintock...using every union tactic of the past" and concluded with the original notion that "if it looks like a duck, waddles like a duck and swims like a duck, it's probably a duck."[19] Other attempts to impugn AIWA's motives in the campaign included ads from the McClintock organization accusing AIWA of a blatant shakedown and letters to AIWA supporters asking if justice were "being coerced into paying debts owed by other firms and being intimidated into signing contracts with non-existent firms."[20]

McClintock Inc. also spread around the "fragrant grease" of corporate largesse to solve the company's growing public relations problem without addressing the fundamental issues raised by the seamstresses. First, investing in the development of an "ethnic ally," McClintock Inc. contributed money to the development of the Northern California Chinese Contractors Association, whose president, Patrick Cheung, has become McClintock Inc.'s "face" in the Asian community. Although Cheung's initial tasks were simply to discredit AIWA and intimidate the seamstresses, his duties expanded to those of a political "bagman" as the contractors association became the chosen entity to pass through "charitable contributions" from McClintock Inc. to the seamstresses. When seven of them refused the money, it was offered to key organizations in the Bay Area Asian community. The director of one of the organizations that received an unsolicited donation, the Asian Women's Shelter, returned the money to McClintock Inc. and stated in a public conference that McClintock was "trying to buy off the community or at least split the community over this issue."[21]

McClintock Inc. also tried to intimidate and co-opt the seamstresses themselves. They videotaped and photographed campaign events, published the women's names in the Chinese press, placed harassing phone calls, fired a seamstress photographed participating in a campaign rally, held "subtle" discussions with relatives of the seamstresses, and blacklisted the seamstresses who stood up for back wages. These are just a few of the tactics used to "motivate" the women to discontinue their efforts.

Probably McClintock's most effective counter-organizing effort was the "velvet glove" approach of the model contract. The Department of Labor, working with an industry organization, San Francisco Fashion Industries, and a McClintock-supported contractors' association, announced the development of a model contract that would provide, in the words of Labor Secretary Robert Reich, "the payment of fair wages for workers and a fair profit for manufacturers and contractors."[22]

According to AIWA organizers, the contractors' association endorsed the contract because they were assured by local Department of Labor staff that signing it would cut down on "hot goods" raids on their shops.[23] Laws governing hot goods (those produced in violation of federal minimum wage, overtime, or child labor laws) permit federal officials to obtain a court injunction prohibiting transport of the goods. Companies are able to resume shipments after they pay all back wages owed to workers.[24] After an appeal by AIWA, federal Department of Labor officials publicly asserted that signing the model contract did not guarantee immunity from raids. Contractor enthusiasm waned noticeably. In addition, attorneys at the San Francisco-based Asian Law Caucus, an organization with decades of experience representing garment workers, found that the model contract "does nothing to ensure high enough (piecework) prices for workers to earn minimum wages and to shorten their long work days."[25]

Getting Results

Why has McClintock Inc. spent over a million dollars to *not* pay twelve seamstresses $15,000? The question is clearly not money. Is it really a matter of principle? Obviously not, since the company has offered the women charitable contributions that would more than cover the wages. The conflict between McClintock Inc. and twelve seamstresses was much more fundamentally about power and precedent.

More at stake than the wages themselves is whether manufacturers should be liable for wages that the contractors they hire owe to workers. The apparel industry was dead set against McClintock Inc. paying the seamstresses' wages because it would have set a precedent that all manufacturers would have had to live with. If AIWA wins against McClintock, their victory will open the door to other organizing campaigns seeking to hold manufacturers accountable to workers who work for contractors like Lucky Sewing.

By the end of 1995, Jessica McClintock Inc. had not paid the seamstresses their back wages. Still, the campaign had significant results in a number of arenas. An initial effect of the campaign was that it made the plight of garment workers publicly visible. Because the campaign spotlighted the plight of twelve individual women, it allowed organizers to develop a public perception of the day-to-day realities of the garment industry. The fingers that sew the clothes are no longer invisible. And, because McClintock Inc. was attempting to distance itself from the contractor, the company never refuted the descriptions of unsafe conditions and poor wages that permeate the apparel industry. AIWA advanced a litany of unanswered charges. Therefore, although McClintock conceded no legal liability, in the public eye McClintock Inc. was still morally responsible for the seamstresses' genuine grievances.

Another direct result of the campaign is that a number of local municipalities have started investigating Bay Area sweatshops. Coupled with the development of a "weak, but worth fighting to improve" model contract, the creation of a special $815,000 fund for garment workers' back wages administered by the California Department of Industrial Relations, and the continuation of "hot goods" raids, Bay Area garment shops are starting to get some scrutiny and garment workers finally have some avenues to redress their grievances. These accomplishments should not be underestimated. The Department of Labor began to seriously enforce wage and hour laws in sweatshops only after the campaign was initiated. Before the campaign, state actions resulted in charges being filed against the garment workers, not in pressure on the employers.[26]

The campaign's ability to economically pressure and publicly embarrass McClintock Inc. was greatly enhanced by the development of a national campaign infrastructure. This patchwork quilt of local operations comprised of students, community activists, labor organizations, women's groups, and Asian service agencies succeeded in forcing McClintock Inc. to reply to charges of injustice by taking out newspaper ads, appearing on radio talk shows, and writing op-ed pieces in the Asian press. [27]The picketing actions were not only effective in stirring up public opinion, they also hurt sales in both the San Francisco and Los Angeles stores, where sales were reported to be down by 30 percent.[28] In addition, local activists in Boston and Los Angeles were able to use the energy generated by the campaign to raise issues about the working conditions for garment workers in their cities.

The campaign transformed AIWA. Principally a service organization for Asian women immigrants, the campaign increased the organization's capacity a hundredfold. Not only does the organization have a Bay Area base of volunteers numbering over 300 individuals and fifty organizations, the organization's style of operation has changed tremendously. AIWA has developed a network of research assistants and connections in scores of women's, labor, church-based, student, and community organizations. Though the staff is still small, with six full-time paid positions, the office is alive with volunteers conducting interviews with workers in three languages, researching the garment and electronics industries, and planning upcoming events. AIWA is also developing a donor base which includes both students who have participated in the campaign and middle-class women who have donated their dresses and their dollars to AIWA actions. In describing the difference in organizational activity, Young Shin sighs, "It's almost never quiet."

The most important result of AIWA's efforts may well be the shining example of an issue campaign that principally affects Asian women being defined, refined, initiated, and followed through by Asian women themselves. As organizer Ken Fong observed, "Before the campaign, the women had a lot of fear and the fear kept them from speaking. Now, even though many of the women are still afraid, they do speak out." The campaign became a training ground for a new generation of Asian women activists. Hundreds of young women have learned valuable skills that they'll use to build power and presence in their communities.

As this book was going to press, Jessica McClintock agreed to AIWA's demands. McClintock agreed to pay each worker $10,000, fund an organization and hotline to help government workers, and contract only with fully bonded factories.

Chapter Six

Contesting the Price of Mexican Labor

Immigrant Workers Fight for Justice

by David Bacon

At the end of the 19th century a wave of labor unrest, massive strikes and class conflict swept across America. Most of the workers involved in these labor actions toiled on the bottom of the economic ladder—picking cotton and cutting sugar cane, digging ditches, building roads, mining coal and sulfur—laboring under the worst conditions and for the lowest pay. A great many workers and leaders of working-class rebellions were immigrants. They brought their traditions and politics with them when they came to America. German socialists, Jewish Marxists from Eastern Europe, Italian and Spanish anarcho-syndicalists, and many others made their contributions to the fierce struggles that laid the foundation for contemporary labor organizations.

At the end of the twentieth century, a similar process is under way, most notably in states with a high percentage of recent immigrants from Mexico and Central America. In California, where the passage of an anti-immigrant state ballot initiative called Proposition 187 in 1994 electrified immigrant communities, labor struggles involving recent immigrants confront the traditional policies and tactics of the labor movement and provide a new basis for its survival and growth. Immigrants from south of the border have brought a tradition of militant organizing, an unwillingness to simply sit by in the face of exploitation, and sometimes a deep connection to labor struggles in their countries of origin. They have also led the way in building strong connections between the community and the workplace, between their struggles as workers and their struggles as students, neighbors, and parents.

Through these struggles, immigrant workers are directly challenging some of the powerful economic trends that have been transforming American society, usually to the detriment of working-class wages and living standards. Immigrants are at the forefront of struggles against the vast expansion of subcontracting, the ability of corporations to quickly shift production to other regions or countries, severe downward pressure on wages in many industries, the decline of unionization, and toxic contamination of residential neighborhoods by industry.

In California and other high-immigration states like Florida, Texas, and New York, immigration status provides a common ground, defining the unique relationship immigrants (especially undocumented immigrants) have to employers, unions, and other institutions. Although closely tied to language, class, and culture in specific areas, immigration status is also a unifying connection between people of different ethnic, language, and cultural backgrounds. It often denotes both a high level of exploitation and a surprising degree of militancy and organization.[1]

Backbone of Labor Action

In the 1980s and 1990s in California, immigrant workers were the backbone of nearly every strike in some of the hardest-fought labor struggles since the farm workers' battles of the late 1960s. Throughout California and the southwest, factories and workplaces have become pressure cookers, waiting for something to blow. Caught between the insatiable demands of modern production methods and the desire for decent jobs and lives, drywallers, framers, grape pickers, janitors, garment workers, electronics assemblers, foundry and metal workers, and many others have "blown out," striking for better wages and working conditions.

Over 20,000 workers walked off their jobs or participated in organizing campaigns between 1990 and 1995. Their strikes are signs of pressure building from below, as the growing dissatisfaction of immigrant workers meets an increasingly hard line taken by the employers who have grown dependent on their labor.

These job actions have rocked the foundation of those industries in the state whose economy depends on them. It's no accident that California's southland, the political home of Republican Governor Pete Wilson and the center of these strikes, has also been the source of most of the Republican proposals for restricting the rights of immigrant workers and services to immigrant communities. But as anti-immigrant hysteria rises, even liberal Democrats have come forward with their own proposals.

In the eyes of immigrants themselves, these proposals are not only racist but reflect a desire to keep immigrants trapped in low-wage jobs. José Semperio, director of San Francisco's Comité de Trabajadores Generales, a committee of day laborers who get their jobs on street corners every morning, points out that as the immigrant population has grown the immigrant community has become increasingly marginalized. "San Francisco, Los Angeles, San Diego, and Orange County all eat because we work. But we have almost no chance to move upwards into better jobs, and to get out of the shadows. These proposals oppress us even more."[2]

Without immigrant janitors in the office and business parks of Century City, without farm workers in southern California fields, with no electronics workers in the sweatshops of Santa Ana, and without immigrant dishwashers and room cleaners in the luxury hotels of Newport Beach, the economy of southern California would crumble. Immigrants are indispensable to the economy of those areas where the cry for exclusion is the strongest.

Semperio accuses the proponents of anti-immigrant measures of hypocrisy, since the communities and businesses they represent benefit heavily from low-wage immigrant labor. "They have an economic interest in what they're proposing," he says. He describes the high accident rate among construction day laborers, almost all of whom are immigrants, and the almost-insurmountable barriers they face when trying to get medical attention. "Already when we have accidents, we're just dropped off at the hospital parking lot. Now they want to make it illegal for us to get medical care [Prop187 denies medical care to undocumented immigrants]. This is really unjust. Our voice may not be as loud, but they're going to have to hear it."

During the height of the debate over the Immigration Reform and Control Act in the early 1980s, the well-known Mexican demographer Jorge Bustamante declared that the purpose of U.S. immigration legislation was always regulating the price of Mexican labor in the United States. This growing wave of labor unrest is putting the lie to the notion that immigrants will settle for the lowest wages and conditions possible. Fabian Nuñez, a spokesperson for the Mexican-American Political Association in Pomona, says current anti-immigrant proposals "are only trying to keep the lid on."

The New Majority

Anti-immigrant hysteria also reflects changing demographics in the workforce and in urban communities throughout California. Pomona, for instance, was one of the original white-flight suburbs of Los Angeles, a defense and aerospace town, with big plants employing thousands of workers at high wages. Many of those plants have now closed. White people are not the majority in Pomona any longer, and Mexican immigrants are a large, growing, and vocal community. In 1993, the town was shaken by a bitter strike that paralyzed what is now its largest employer, Cal Spas, a vast industrial sweatshop making spas and hot tubs for upper-middle-class homes.

Southern California's economy, once home to massive automobile and rubber factories, steel mills, and other heavy industries, now depends more on industries like home-building and improvement, garment manufacturing, agriculture, and tourism. These industries in turn depend on immigrant labor, and they are increasingly marked by strikes over sweatshop conditions.

Throughout 1992, the southern California construction industry was rocked by the successful strike of 5,000 "drywalleros," the Mexican workers who do the backbreaking job of nailing up drywall in new homes. The workers demanded an increase in the piece rate, which had fallen by more than 50 percent over the previous ten years. Border patrol agents repeatedly raided drywall picket lines. When the Highway Patrol harassed carloads of strikers as they moved their picket lines from one building site to another, strikers protested by blocking freeways, the lifelines of southern California.

In 1993, the drywallers finally forced building contractors to sign contracts. They were the first union contracts covering drywall work in decades. They were also the first union contracts won by an independent union organizing effort in the building trades anywhere in the country since the 1930s. In the spring of 1995, the scenario was repeated by 2,000 immigrant framers, the carpenters who put up the wooden skeletons in houses.

These strikes electrified unions and workers across the Southwest, and set new rules for the conduct of successful labor battles. Workers ran these campaigns democratically, from the bottom up. The initial battle of the drywallers won deep respect and support from unions and workers throughout the state, who sent food caravans and money to keep it going.

Drywallers defied the police and the immigration service, and refused to either play by the rules or be intimidated by the constant law enforcement presence. Picketing in the framers' strike broke the stereotypic image of a few strikers with picket signs standing beside a driveway, watching strikebreakers take their jobs. When the framers picketed, their lines numbered in the dozens, and even in the hundreds. They ignored legal restrications on trespassing, picketing, handing out flyers, and other activities. They displayed almost a missionary zeal. Rather than waste their time hurling insults at replacement workers, they walked onto the job sites, stopped the work, and explained to the replacements why they too should join the strike.

These were scenes were reminiscent of the early days of the labor movement, when the radical "Wobblies" of the Industrial Workers of the World at the turn of the century proposed "one big union" for everyone. Mass picket lines, class-conscious organizing, and flying squads of strikers were common tactics used by the Congress of Industrial Organizations (CIO) of the 1930s. Most union locals in this country haven't tried creative rank and file methods like these in many decades, which is one reason organized labor has become increasingly unable to organize and defend jobs and wages.

In a world where workers and unions have become hamstrung following legalistic procedures, on a playing field where only employers win, immigrants like the drywallers and framers are doing the unexpected. They have faith in the power of their own numbers, in direct action, and in the common culture which strikers and non-strikers share. Their strikes were more than just labor disputes. They had the feeling of uprisings from below—challenges to anti-immigrant hysteria and to the politicians and corporations that feed on anti-immigrant sentiment while profiting from cheap immigrant labor.

Organizing and Rebellion

The importance of this wave of immigrant-based labor activity hasn't been lost on those labor activists and organizers trying to find a new constituency for unions, and strategy and tactics appropriate for what many of them describe as "class war." AFL-CIO unions in building services, hotels and restaurants, garment production, and light industries have rebuilt themselves in California by tying their organizing strategy to this upsurge. Based on that experience, unions are now preparing to take on the reorganization of the southern California industrial workforce. Their plan is called the Los Angeles Manufacturing Action Project (LAMAP).

Despite two decades of plant closures, and the loss of most of its heavy industry, Los Angeles is still the largest manufacturing center in the United States. Seven hundred seventeen thousand workers walk through the gates of L.A.'s factories every day, dwarfing the 400,000-strong industrial workforce of Chicago's Cook County, the nation's second largest manufacturing center. Over half of L.A.'s industrial workers are immigrants.

LAMAP director Peter Olney describes the project in deceptively simple terms: "a multi-union, area-wide organizing drive, linked to the immigrant community." Olney believes that the labor movement has been dying because of its disconnection to the social upheavals that gave it birth. Organizing drives, which once moved millions to redress the fundamental inequalities of a corporate economic system, have been forced into mechanical and legalistic campaigns, littered with fired workers, closed plants, and broken unions, where the company holds all the cards.

But the recent history of the union struggles of immigrant workers in Los Angeles is by and large a history of success. "That's the excitement of L.A.," Olney says. "Fights involving immigrant workers are very militant. They've forced unions to discard tired old tactics. They hold out the potential to force us to relook at the whole question of how to organize, and what organizing means."

LAMAP plans to follow the immigrant workforce through the plants and barrios of the nation's largest manufacturing district—the Alameda corridor—sparking a wave of organizing down its length, and targeting industries rather than workplaces. It seeks to build a movement that will sweep through residential communities at the same time, tying the fight for living wages and safe jobs to an end to toxic pollution in schoolyards and neighborhoods. Part of what gives social justice struggles involving immigrants their power and vitality is the lack of separation between community issues and workplace issues; indeed some labor activists argue that organizing around neighborhood issues should be considered another facet of labor organizing.

David Sickler, director of Region 6 of the AFL-CIO, criticizes unions for having been too slow to forge community alliances in the past. "We've organized in a vacuum," he asserts. "By the time we got in fights with a company, and went to get community support, it was already too late. The employer was seen as more of a resident of the community than the workers." Sickler laments "too many years when we walked in lockstep with the NLRB [National Labor Relations Board], organizing one shop at a time. It was a failed approach. I don't think we have any choice other than to change. "Immigrants are our future."

High-Tech Sweatshops

In northern California's largest immigrant community, Silicon Valley, unions have come to the same conclusion. Working life in Silicon Valley has become problematic for thousands of people. While living standards rise for a privileged elite at the top of the workforce, they drop for thousands of workers on the production line. Tens of thousands of workers have been dropped off the line entirely, as production leaves the valley for other states and countries, while companies eliminate their historic no-layoff pledge. Permanent jobs have become temporary. The image of the clean industry has been replaced by the specter of toxic contamination of the valley's water supply, and a high occurrence of chemically-induced industrial illness.

Conditions for janitors and contract assemblers are a far cry from those associated in the public mind with high-tech manufacturing. Paid close to minimum wage, they have no medical insurance, and often no benefits at all. The decline in living standards has made the service and sweatshop economy the focus for organizing activity. Silicon Valley's high-tech workers are finding important new tactics for organizing to oppose these conditions. Some groups, like janitors, have wielded these techniques with remarkable success, winning groundbreaking achievements. For others, especially production workers in the plants themselves, the road seems longer and harder.

The spark that set off this new wave of organizing was the campaign to organize the janitors at Shine Maintenance Co., a contractor hired by Apple Computer Corp. to clean its huge Silicon Valley headquarters. In the fall of 1990, when Shine became aware that its workers had organized, it suddenly demanded proof of their legal residence, citing the employer sanctions provision of the Immigration Reform and Control Act.

The company's actions ignited a year-long campaign, that culminated in the signing of a contract for Apple janitors in 1992. After the company fired workers, the union called a meeting of activist, church, and political figures in San Jose's large Latino community. "We told them that we had taken our struggle as far as we could—that the labor movement is limited because the law hurts workers who want to organize more than it helps them," explained Mike Garcia, president of Silicon Valley's SEIU Local 1877. "So a community coalition went to picket when our union couldn't, supported the workers with a hunger strike, and started a boycott of Apple products." That community effort grew into the Cleaning Up Silicon Valley Coalition, which went on to support the organizing efforts of workers in other companies and other unions.

Using the same strategy, the union won a contract for janitors who clean the headquarters of Hewlett-Packard Corp., an even larger group than those at Apple. The momentum created in those campaigns convinced other non-union janitorial contractors to actively seek agreements with Local 1877, and over 1,500 new members have streamed into the union.

In September of 1992, janitors were joined by electronics assembly workers at Versatronex Corp., who used a similar strategy to organize against the sweatshop conditions prevalent in contract assembly factories. Sergio Mendoza worked in the "coil room," making electrical coils for IBM computers for seven years. The work process involved dipping the coils into chemical baths and drying them off in ovens. "They never told us the names or the dangers of the chemicals we worked with," he recalls. "Sometimes the vapors were so strong that our noses would begin to bleed."

The conditions in the "coil room" are very different from those at IBM's own facilities in South San Jose, which it refers to as a "campus." IBM's orders gave a big boost to Versatronex' contract assembly business over the company's twenty-year history, and workers recall seeing IBM inspectors frequently visiting their plant. Subcontracting provides a number of benefits for large manufacturers like IBM. Assembly contractors compete to win orders by cutting their prices, and workers' wages, to the lowest level possible. Manufacturers can place new orders on a moment's notice when production demands increase, without having to hire any workers themselves. When production needs decrease, they simply cut orders. The primary manufacturer thus has no legal responsibility for any of the workers in the contracting firm, and the contractors themselves are notoriously hard to organize because they simply move or go out of business when faced with an organizing drive.

Workers at Versatronex called in the independent United Electrical Workers (UE), after they had already organized themselves to protest these conditions and as they were preparing to stop work to demand changes. When the company heard rumors of the impending stoppage, they held a meeting to head off the planned action. One worker, Joselito Muñoz, stood up in the meeting and declared to company supervisors that "se acabó el tiempo de la esclavitud," or "the time of slavery is over." Muñoz was fired two days later, and on October 16, 1992, Verstronex workers went on strike to win his job back.

At the high point of the six-week Versatronex strike, ten women strikers went on a hunger strike outside the glittering offices of the company's main customer. Their fast dramatized their effort to hold the manufacturer responsible for their working conditions. Male strikers supported them by setting up tents and living around the clock on the sidewalk.

In the course of the strike, the workers and the union used many tactics drawn from the experiences workers brought with them from Mexico, including the hunger strike. "It is not uncommon for workers in Mexico to fast and set up 'plantons'—tent encampments where workers live for the strike's duration," according to Maria Pantoja, a UE organizer and Mexico City native. "Even striking over the firing of another worker is a reflection of our culture of mutual support, which workers bring with them to this country. Our culture is a source of strength for our union."

But immigrants also have a harder time standing up for their rights in front of the employer, and often are unaware of their rights as workers. Sanctions and the threat of deportation make the risk of losing a job much higher for immigrants than for other workers. These are primary reasons why Justice for Janitors, the national organizing strategy of the Service Employees International Union, doesn't rely on elections administered by the National Labor Relations Board. Instead, the union combines intense community pressure with an all-out attack on the parent corporation. Marches, demonstrations, sit-ins, and other mass actions mobilize the pressure of workers and supporters against the employer.

Tactics like those used at Apple and Versatronex are at the cutting edge of the labor movement's search for new ways to organize. They rely strongly on close alliances among workers, unions, and communities to offset the power exercised by employers. As workers organize around conditions they face on the job, they also deal with issues of immigration, discrimination in the schools, police misconduct, and many others which are part of daily life in immigrant communities. By defining labor issues as essentially community issues, immigrants have been able to build strong coalitions with other social justice organizations working on issues such as education, health care, police accountability, and immigrant rights.

Conflict Over Rights

But the alliance between unions and immigrant workers has also been marked by conflict over the rights those workers have once they become union members, and their ability to exercise leadership in the organization they've joined. The conflict was particularly sharp in the Los Angeles janitors union, Service Employees Local 399.

Local 399 is one of the labor movement's success stories. In the mid-1980s, the city's big real estate and development interests effectively broke the union in building services, using the enormous influx of immigrant workers from Mexico and Central America as a union-busting wedge. But Local 399 organizers retaliated by using tactics developed by Justice for Janitors. In Los Angeles, these tactics relied on the militancy of immigrant workers, and the local's organizers brought them into the streets again and again to win contracts.

Substituting confrontation for labor board elections, they mounted demonstrations, sit-ins, and civil disobedience in building lobbies, blocked traffic on major thoroughfares, and went after the whole industry instead of individual employers. It's hard to imagine these tactics appealing to software designers or other more highly-paid occupations with a more native-born and anglo workforce. But they drew on the traditions and experience of workers who faced down government terror in El Salvador or Guatamala. They appealed to workers who learned, as children do in Mexico, that while they have a right to a fair share of the wealth of society, they have to fight to get it.

Eliseo Medina, head of the janitors union in San Diego, SEIU Local 102, and past vice president of the United Farm Workers, puts it this way: "When you come from a country where they shoot you for being a unionist or a striker, then getting fired from your job doesn't seem so bad. Immigrants from Central America have a much more militant history as unionists than we do, and the more militant workers are, the more the union can do."

When the Los Angeles Police Department brutally beat immigrant janitors who were protesting peacefully among the skyscrapers of Century City, the resulting public outcry gave Local 399 the support it needed to beat the building owners. But the victory, sweet as it was, opened the doors to tensions between the new members and the longstanding union structure. In June 1995, a group of janitors formed an alliance with other union members working in hospitals. They called their new network the Multiracial Alliance. In the union election held that month, the Multiracial Alliance ran a slate of candidates for the union's executive board. Alliance candidates won every position except one—union president. Local 399's president for almost two decades, Jim Zellers, ran unopposed, but the slate of candidates which he supported was defeated.

Afterwards, the new executive board tried to fire the union's lawyers and staff members who the board claimed were not representing members adequately. Zellers blocked the board's action. The internal workings of the union broke down.

On August 3, twelve workers began a hunger strike in front of the union's offices in downtown L.A., using the same tactics against their union that they had used to fight the big Los Angeles building owners. For eighteen days they lived in tents pitched on a narrow strip of dirt between the walls of the union hall and the sidewalk. Banners calling for union democracy were draped in the trees next to the street, and crowds of workers supporting both Zellers and the hunger strikers swirled around the union hall. After a series of unfruitful negotiations, the Service Employees headquarters appointed a trustee to run the local, Mike Garcia of Silicon Valley's SEIU Local 1877.

The militant traditions of immigrant workers served the union well as a source of anger and energy directed against employers. But they also carried with them the expectation that workers would have a significant amount of control over their union once they were members of it. Many janitors felt these expectations were unfulfilled. "Organizers treated us as cannon fodder," Multiracial Alliance leader Cesar Oliva charges, "pushing us forward, but not permitting us to make decisions over the process."

That point makes the local's problem relevant to other unions, especially those in California and the Southwest who also see immigrant workers as the base for a new upsurge in power and militancy. Unions find that when these workers join, especially as a result of hard-fought battles which bring out their combativeness and raise their expectations, these new members want a say in how their union is run. They want control over contract negotiations and grievance handling.

That can threaten the delicate balance of power inside any union, not to mention the jobs of union staff.

For Latino workers, unions have become an indispensable tool for winning political power in California. That is a survival question in the era of Proposition 187, and one which places them squarely in the mainstream of the U.S. labor tradition for immigrant workers. But they are also coming into unions whose structure and power are held by an already entrenched leadership. Immigrants sometimes find that they have to win power inside their unions before they can use the union structure to fight for broader goals.

Connecting with Community

Immigrant-based labor struggles are also forming important alliances with other community-based movements, especially those organizing against environmental racism and discrimination in the schools. LAMAP itself is an alliance between unions and one of L.A.'s most respected grassroots environmental organizations, Citizens for a Better Environment (CBE). CBE changed its name in 1995 to Communities for a Better Environment because organizers found that the word "citizen" excluded much of their hoped-for constituency among recent immigrants. It is one of California's most aggressive environmental organizations, with a long history of suing and fighting corporations over toxic contamination. Unlike many other environmental advocates, it has good relations with unions, and a record of balancing concern over jobs and the health of workers with cleaning up pollution.

In 1994 CBE moved its offices out of the outlying city of Venice and into the old Standard Oil Building in downtown Los Angeles. Then it hired Carlos Porras as CBE's southern California director to organize the barrios along the Alameda corridor against some of the highest levels of toxic pollution in the country.

It was a wrenching change in some ways. Huntington Park Mayor Rick Loya, who was on the CBE board at the time, says that "for some in the environmental community, fish come first. But CBE has expertise that minority communities need, especially small cities and communities who don't have a lot of resources of their own." Porras calls it "a conscious decision to get grounded as an organization in communities which have become L.A.'s toxic hotspots." Porras and CBE started LA CAUSA—Los Angeles Comunidades Assembladas y Unidas para un Sostenable Ambiente (Los Angeles Communities Assembled in Unity for a Sustainable Environment).

Their first community organizing effort took on Aggregate Recycling Systems, a concrete recycling company, which had erected a mountain of discarded concrete in a residential neighborhood in Huntington Park. Concrete dust and noise are not as toxic as some of the other pollutants coming from the factories of the Alameda corridor. But LA CAUSA understood that its visibility to the residents of the neighborhood, and the misery it causes them, made the issue a community rallying cry.

LA CAUSA organized the neighbors behind the mountain of concrete to contest the facility's use permit before the city council. LA CAUSA arranged to have an air dispersion study made. It showed unacceptably high levels of airborne particulates, which are dust particles too small to be seen, but which cause the most damage to the lungs. Huntington Park's planning commission received the study, but refused to accept its conclusions, or to conduct an environmental impact review of its own. The city voted to study the matter further, but wouldn't stop the recycler's operation.

While Mayor Loya was sympathetic, other council members clearly weren't. "You see," says Porras, "there's a lot of political turmoil in southeast L.A., which has given us some new Latino faces in city governments here, which before were almost exclusively white. But often we've replaced the white defenders of industry with Latino defenders of industry. I can't say we have a really progressive government in any city here. We got involved in the Aggregate hearings because of the rampant pro-business mentality which exists in Huntington Park, and in all the cities of the Alameda corridor."

Neighborhood outrage provides an opportunity for LA CAUSA to build its base in the immigrant community and workforce, by taking on the issues that provoke spontaneous protest over an immediate environmental threat. LA CAUSA organizes its community base in gritty struggles, factory by factory, neighborhood by neighborhood. Its strategy is to use that base to challenge even more serious environmental problems.

Porras believes that no matter how important the issue, it's too hard to mobilize people against abstract policy questions. LA CAUSA begins, therefore, with the issues which are the most visible to people in the community. Fighting Aggregate Recycling Systems is seen as a step towards larger struggles, like building a campaign against the Air Quality Management District (an official agency in charge of allocating pollution "credits" that tends to concentrate polluting industries in immigrant neighborhoods). Together, they are part of an overall strategy to build a movement against toxic racism and for environmental justice in the immigrant communities of the Alameda corridor.

"We want to articulate an industry-wide and area-wide policy which reduces toxics and prevents pollution," Porras says. "It's going to take site-specific struggles to get us there." He looks to a long-term alliance especially with the city's labor movement to provide the political muscle to challenge industry power in local governments.

Porras explains that increasing the power of immigrants at work will ultimately make it easier for them to win their efforts to clean up their neighborhoods. "The environment is not the number one need in people's lives," he says. "People have to sustain themselves first. Once they've started to climb the economic ladder, they start articulating demands for a better environment to live in." LAMAP's Peter Olney responds that "our issue isn't job creation; it's control of the labor market. Communities represented by unions can use that control to raise their economic level and win political power." LA CAUSA actively supports union drives, members walk picket lines, and the group brings community pressure to bear on employers when workers need the leverage.

Similarly powerful connections are being made between education fights and labor struggles. In outrage over Proposition 187, thousands of high school students walked out of classes and marched through city streets behind the Mexican flag and banners which read "No Human Being Is Illegal." These anti-187 protests began in the San Francisco Bay Area, and spread to other parts of northern California. By they time they reached Los Angeles, thousands were "blowing out" of school.

These marches had their roots in two years of similar school strikes, protesting discrimination against Chicano and Latino students and the lack of school curricula addressing their experience. According to Gabriel Hernandez, an organizer for the Hotel Employees and Restaurant Employees (HERE) Local 2850 in Oakland, who helped the students to organize, "These young people just don't see anything out there for them. Reaganomics sliced and diced away the facade that anyone gives a damn about them, and this generation is really angry. At least they found a way to say what they felt about it."

Many of the student demonstrations were organized by the Student Empowerment Program (StEP), started by Chicano Moratorium activists. StEP formed committees in high schools, planning outreach, publicity, and logistics for demonstrations. José Lopez, a college StEP organizer, says, "We don't want students to walk out and then go off by themselves. We hold a rally and teach for the day. When they first walk out, students may not fully know why they're doing it. By the end of the day they will—that's assured. There are no adults, just high school students talking to each other."[3] There was no violence during the walk-outs; young people put gang and turf affiliations aside by appealing to larger identities as immigrants and students.

Hernandez saw the chance to teach young people skills they could not only use to organize their protests over anti-immigrant hysteria, but take with them into other aspects of their lives. "My job is to help them hook up—hook up with each other, hook up their issues with those of other people, hook up their own ideas to a bigger picture of the world, and hook up to unions too. Now, when I get them to participate in a union organizing drive, they get it right away. They're doing something they already know how to do. They know how to talk about fear. They can see that it takes numbers to win, whether it's winning a union vote or shutting down a freeway to protest 187."

Many veterans of the StEP blow-outs now help Hernandez' union to organize the immigrant workers at the Park Hotel in Lafayette, in one of the San Francisco Bay Area's wealthiest communities.

Back Over the Border

As the debate over the North American Free Trade Agreement (NAFTA) rolled across the country in 1992 and 1993, labor activists started worrying about rapidly accelerating job losses. Cross-border organizing became one of the most hotly-discussed ideas among progressive activists.

The idea is not really new. The Flores Magon brothers planned the first battles of the Mexican revolution with supporters from the Wobblies in St. Louis and Los Angeles, and paid for threatening U.S. mining interests with imprisonment and death in Leavenworth. In the heady days of the CIO, Vicente Lombardo Toledano and Latin American labor radicals built ties between progressive union federations from Canada to Central America.

These traditions were largely forgotten, as Cold War defense of U.S. foreign policy and corporate interests, and hostility to immigrants and radicals, were promoted by the international apparatus of the AFL-CIO after World War II. When NAFTA created a crisis calling for a common front of labor in the U.S., Canada, and Mexico, workers and unions had to start building this front from scratch. While immigrant-based activism has been a product of the immigration of millions of working people from Mexico and Central America, in one of the great ironies of the global economy, it has spilled back over the border into Mexico. Even before the passage of NAFTA, the growth of maquiladoras just south of Texas, New Mexico, Arizona, and California led to the flight of thousands of jobs out of the U.S. In the Southwest, those have been overwhelmingly jobs done by immigrants themselves.

In 1984, immigrant women in the giant freezers of Watsonville Canning and Frozen Foods fought an epic, 19-month strike that reformed and saved their union, Local 912 of the International Brotherhood of Teamsters. But in the years following, most of the freezers in Watsonville reduced their workforce, moved production, and closed. Finally, the Green Giant broccoli freezer, the local's largest employer, relocated its operations to the Mexican state of Irapuato.

Building on the tradition of activism in their union, immigrant workers, mostly women, formed Trabajadores Desplazados, or Displaced Workers. In addition to fighting for severance pay and retraining, they took an unprecedented step. A delegation of workers and local leaders went to Irapuato and made contact with an independent Mexican union, the Authentic Labor Front (FAT). Together, they mounted a long campaign against Green Giant's corporate parent and eventually won better displacement benefits in Watsonville, and forced the company to clean up toxic plant discharges in Mexico.

While Congress was debating NAFTA in 1993, the women of Watsonville became part of a larger movement of working women all along the border, dealing with the same problems of job flight and free trade. In San Antonio, Texas, over 1,000 women were laid off by Levi-Strauss when it closed a large plant and moved south. They responded by forming Fuerza Unida (United Force). They fought for more severance and better retraining, and in national tours and fasts designed to bring publicity to their case, they became symbols of how easily workers are discarded in the global marketplace for labor.

In El Paso, Texas, women garment workers formed La Mujer Obrera (The Woman Worker) to help women in the mostly-unorganized garment sweatshops. Trying to overcome the historically low percentage of unionized employers in El Paso, and the consequent low incomes for the families of garment workers, they assisted organizers from the International Ladies Garment Workers Union. The relationship was rocky, and a leader of La Mujer says bitterly that AFL-CIO unions "don't care about our problems. As long as they get their own salaries, why bother to organize?"

On the night NAFTA passed, women from La Mujer Obrera marched to the middle of the international bridge connecting El Paso and Ciudad Juarez, protesting the corporate priorities of free trade and mistreatment at the hands of authorities on both sides of the border. They sat down and refused to move until they were threatened with arrest by the Border Patrol. Like Fuerza Unida, La Mujer Obrera has been forced to deal with the closure of garment factories all over the city. Carmen Ibarra, a La Mujer leader: "We can't pretend we can stop companies from moving out of El Paso. We know this is bigger than us, but what we can do is mobilize pressure to respond to the plant closures."[4]

Efforts to develop working relations with unions and workers in Mexico have sprouted all along the border, from Brownsville and Matamoros to San Diego and Tijuana, during and after the NAFTA debate. The UE and the Teamsters formed a cooperative organizing relationship with the FAT, to try to organize unions in border factories in Juarez and Chihuahua. The Coalition for Justice in the Maquiladoras helped workers at Sony's Nuevo Laredo plant fight to democratize their union. And in San Diego, union activists in the Committee to Support Maquiladora Workers help the Tijuana-based Border Workers Regional Support Committee organize classes for maquiladora workers, training them in ways of conducting guerrilla health and safety campaigns in their plants. All of these organizations have long histories of being outspoken advocates of the rights of immigrants in the U.S. as well.

The connection is not hard to see. Just south of San Ysidro, or El Paso, or Brownsville, "workers work for incredibly low wages," according to organizer Eduardo Badillo. "They earn $3 for an eight-hour day, when the same business in the U.S. pays workers $5 for a single hour, even if those workers are not legal immigrants. Here a worker can't earn that same five dollars with a whole day's work."

United by Economics, Divided by a Wall

A ten-foot iron wall separates Tijuana from San Ysidro and extends to the east. Although it stops few people from crossing the border, it is a potent symbol of the U.S. government's attitude towards poor Mexican immigrants. Regardless of the party in power, the federal government is committed to preventing illegal immigration through the use of more Border Patrol agents, and even U.S. troops, armed with the latest high-tech military gadgetry. Their job is to deny hungry people the same free passage that NAFTA extends to money and goods.

But while many U.S. unions have historically been anti-immigration, arguing that waves of cheap illegal labor drive down wages in the United States, the great irony is that—at least in California—it is these immigrants who are transforming and re-energizing the labor movements. While U.S. economic and trade policies in effect encourage them to leave Mexico, U.S. immigration and social welfare policies punish them when they do.

U.S. unions have always been divided about immigration. The progressive and radical tradition, often based among immigrants themselves, called for uniting workers to fight the employers. Unions in this tradition defended immigrants, often when no one else would, and sought to link workers across national borders. But the more conservative tradition sought to exclude immigrants, along with people of color and women generally, and looked at unions as the domain of the privileged and skilled—of white men. Following the purge of radicals in the McCarthyite years of the 1950s, conservatives dominated the leadership of U.S. unions for many years, arguing that cheap immigrant labor was driving down wages.

But over the last two decades in California, and increasingly throughout the country, unions have rediscovered their more radical traditions, as immigrants themselves transform and re-energize a big part of the labor movement. And now that SEIU's president John Sweeney is president of the AFL-CIO, that process might well start to shake up the whole of organized labor, finally putting some "movement" into labor.

"I want to make it clear," says Juan José Delgado of Tijuana's Comité Para Todos. "The Mexicans who emigrate are often the best people, the bravest, most valuable ones. Their educational level is two or three times higher than the average here at home. You in the U.S. should be happy they're coming." U.S. unions have not exactly extended a welcoming hand over the past few decades, but it seems at least possible that big changes are coming.

Chapter Seven

Linking Community Safety with Police Accountability

By John Anner

As the last bloody years of the twentieth century slip away, a key locus of the class struggle in the United States has become the protracted war between the cops and the criminalized. Their labor no longer required by an economy once again in the throes of a disruptive transformation, millions of dispossessed Americans have decided, as they have during other eras, that if they can't be part of the game, then they see no reason to play by the rules.[1] Lacking effective class-based collective political organizations, the marginalized take individual action (or join gangs).[2]

Understanding the meaning of crime and deciding what to do about it is a critical issue for all social justice organizations and movements. The State has two ways to respond to outbreaks of class struggle (whether they are consciously political or not) that lead to instability: repression and co-optation through provision of benefits. Law enforcement and social welfare programs are thus intrinsically linked, and one strategy or another is followed depending on the political circumstances. Piven and Cloward have persuasively argued, for example, that the New Deal was implemented primarily to forestall massive system-threatening social upheaval in the wake of the Great Depression.[3]

Repression is now the rule of the day. But while crime might endanger the social order, it is rarely directed at the rich and powerful. People generally rob and attack those closest to them. The poor prey on others barely making it and Blacks and whites alike for the most part commit crimes against members of their own race. Social disorganization hits hardest at the law-abiding majority living in high-crime areas, and for this reason when the members of those communities who still have a stake in the system get together to improve their communities often the first campaigns they take on are anti-crime and anti-drugs.

This impulse is fully understandable, but it can play into the hands of policymakers eager to pursue the repression strategy of more prisons, more police, and more people behind bars for longer periods of time. As the well-known scholar/activist Clarence Lusane wrote in *Third Force* in early 1995, "Too often the impulse to do something about crime reinforces the very politics that are destroying communities of color."[4]

While there are many organizations, especially in communities of color, organized to resist official violence and repression, there are only a few cases of sustained organizing aimed at both "reducing crime" (i.e., rebuilding community) and stopping the war waged on the poor by the police and the justice system. As the Black Panthers sometimes argued, making this link is a critical political step, because it puts together in the same package elements of community-building and resistance to the depredations of racist capitalism. A significant recent example of such a struggle is the national work of the Campaign for Community Safety and Police Accountability (CCSPA).

A Victory for the People

In a widely-reported press conference held on August 4, 1995, jubilant staff and members of People United for a Better Oakland (PUEBLO) proclaimed that their year-long organizing campaign to redirect law enforcement funds back into community programs had achieved its goal. Deputy Police Chief Tom Donahue announced at the press conference that the Oakland Police Department would henceforth turn over 15 percent of the funds it received under the Asset Forfeiture Fund (AFF) program to Oakland community groups.

Furthermore, a new community board was created to decide which community groups would get the money. Two PUEBLO members were appointed to sit on the board, sharing responsibilities with the Police Department for deciding how to reallocate law enforcement funds to social programs. "We won!" exulted PUEBLO leader Joyce Taylor. "We started this campaign because we were sick and tired of watching our government throwing more tax dollars into more prisons and more police. We believe asset forfeiture money belongs to the community." "The partnership is the first of its kind in the nation," wrote *San Francisco Chronicle* reporter Henry Lee in an April 5 front-page story, "and represents a major departure in the way police departments around the country use money from asset forfeiture programs."[5]

In fact, PUEBLO's victory represents a major departure from the entire debate over crime and punishment in America, which for at least thirty years has featured an increasingly aggressive and expensive program of law enforcement, incarceration, strict sentencing, and expanded police powers. PUEBLO is a member organization of CCSPA. The CCSPA links community groups around the country in a coordinated effort to bring an inner-city perspective to the debate over crime and the role of police and other law enforcement agencies. Its goals are to win victories at the local level and build on these successes to force broader changes, and to link what are usually separate discussions and organizing efforts around police accountability and safe, decent communities.

As Denver resident and CCSPA member Shannon Smith put it in a June 1994 CCSPA press conference held in Washington, D.C., "Everyone should have the right to walk the streets in safety, feel secure in their own home and be able to go out at night without worrying about being robbed, beaten, raped, or killed. Too many of us, however, have as much fear of the police and other law enforcement agents as we do of bandits and law-breakers. Proposals to 'do something about crime' need to take into account that what people really want is to feel safe. Nobody can feel safe living in a community where the police routinely threaten, harass and brutalize the very citizens they are supposed to protect."

Starting from the perspective that crime as a political issue stands at a critical juncture of race and class, CCSPA organizers believe that successfully re-framing law enforcement policies in a progressive direction is one of the key elements in any grassroots struggle for social justice. In many inner cities, the police are perceived as an army of occupation, an external armed force in the pay of the wealthy whose mission is to prevent uprisings and rebellions, both large and small, against daily injustices. The fight for decent lives for the poor and disenfranchised, then, depends on breaking the logic that the severe problems of the city are best dealt with through law enforcement, rather than through a comprehensive network of social services and benefits such as drug treatment, youth programs, school reform, legal services, income support, and the rest of the underfunded programs of the New Deal, Great Society, and War on Poverty.

"Prevention not detention" is the Campaign's unofficial motto, meaning both that resources should be directed into social programs like the ones listed above and that law enforcement agencies need to be held accountable for their actions. Thus, the member organizations of the CCSPA are involved in the campaign on multiple levels, often going after the municipal police both to redirect resources and to "jam them up" around police misconduct. Six months after their joint press conference, for example, PUEBLO members were back in the Oakland Police Department, invading and occupying the department's headquarters for over an hour and demanding an immediate meeting with the Chief. Waving slices of baloney to demonstrate what they thought of the department's promises, PUEBLO members shouted and chanted until a police representative agreed to set up a meeting. This time, however, the community group was not looking for action around the use of Asset Forfeiture funds. Instead, the group was demanding that the department explain why it had not taken any action on over a hundred formal complaints of police abuse and misconduct filed by Oakland residents over the past year.

Making the Connection

Of course, grassroots organizing against both police misconduct and criminality is nothing new. The Black Panthers, for example, got their start fighting racist police practices, and there are various forms of police accountability organizations still active that seek to limit the power of law enforcement agencies, impose some kind of civilian oversight, and/or discipline particularly brutal officers. Especially in communities of color, which have long borne the brunt of police misconduct and harsh incarceration policies, there is a strong tradition of anti-police brutality mobilizing and resistance.

The effectiveness of police accountability activism, however, has been undermined by pro-police arguments that such civilian oversight hampers the police's ability to fight crime, thus making communities even more unsafe. This was the problem that CCSPA organizers confronted when they began developing their plan to halt the explosion in law enforcement that they believed was devouring government budgets and closing off other more progressive policy options. "We are up-front in that we are building a grassroots movement to hold the police accountable for their behavior in our communities," says CCSPA coordinator Francis Calpotura. "As organizers for [social justice], we need to figure out strategies to shift the balance of power from law enforcement to community institutions. At this point, part of what needs to happen is to shift financial resources from punishment to prevention."[6]

Getting Tough on Crime

It's an uphill fight for CCSPA members. To the question of what to do about crime, there has recently been only one public policy answer—more cops, more prison cells, more death sentences, and more onerous time behind bars. The few voices raised in opposition to this trend, such as the Sentencing Project or the Center on Juvenile and Criminal Justice, have been drowned in a tidal wave of proposals designed to "get tough on crime." Curfew laws for young people, mandatory life imprisonment for third or even second felony convictions, expanded lists of crimes eligible for the death penalty, long prison terms for even minor drug convictions and hundreds of others are the law in almost every state.

Deciding to buck this trend and advocate for more social programs instead of more jail cells is a lonely political choice. Few politicians, even liberal ones, are willing to come out and say they would rather have more social spending and far fewer would dare to campaign against a "tough on crime" proposal or candidate. For example, the Clinton administration easily passed a $30 billion crime bill in late 1994, but failed to win even modest new allocations of federal funds for health care reform or urban renewal. The same is true of most community organizations active in the high-crime inner city; indeed, the public perception that crime was out of control—accurate or not—combined with the "war on drugs" in the early 1990s to create a climate in which crime rose to the top of the list of things Americans were most concerned about. Hundreds of new community groups, attempting to "take back the streets" in their neighborhoods, got involved in anti-drug and anti-violence activities of all kinds.

As a result, the pressure from the grassroots in many cities was for an expansion of police activities, an increase in the number of cops walking the streets, stricter sentencing, and fewer limits on police powers. Attempts to also raise issues of police misconduct are generally not appreciated by law enforcement agencies.[7] Individual chapters of national community organizing networks like National People's Action developed "partnerships" with local police departments, setting up various methods of informing the police of suspicious activities in their neighborhoods and encouraging more arrests and a greater police presence. Independent "neighborhood watch" committees were most likely the fastest-growing form of neighborhood organization during the 1990s; by some estimates as many as 16.5 million Americans belonged to some kind of anti-crime group by 1994.

The American Gulag

By any measure, America's prisons and law enforcement agencies have undergone a remarkable expansion over the past few decades. Two million Americans now languish behind bars. Since 1973, the number of individuals in prison has quadrupled, to a 1993 rate of 519 per 100,000, second only to Russia in the world and five to eight times the average rate for Western Europe or Canada.[8] According to the Bureau of Justice Statistics, 5.1 million Americans—or 2.7 percent of the U.S. population—are now behind bars or on parole. "Welcome to America's 51st state," says a brochure put out by the Center on Juvenile and Criminal Justice. "You won't find it on any map. Yet its population is growing faster than any other state in the U.S."

Over half of these convicted offenders are African-American, while African Americans are only twelve percent of the population.[9] There are now more African Americans in prison (583,000) than in college (537,000). For every Latino man with a college degree, 24 of his brothers are behind bars. Sixty percent of all prisoners are African-American or Latino, a proportion that rises significantly for maximum security prisons. California's notorious Pelican Bay state prison, for example, is sixty percent Latino and eighty-seven percent men of color.[10]Thirty percent of young African-American and Latino men in California are in prison, in jail, or on parole.

While the crime rate rose only marginally from 1981 to 1991, from 5.85 percent to 5.89 percent, the rate of incarceration increased 155 percent during that period, mostly fueled by high rates of incarceration for drug crimes.[11] And while nearly all social programs were on the chopping block during the austerity eighties, $90 billion was spent to triple the amount of new prison space, with an estimated $15 billion per year allocated for the rest of the decade.[12] While the percentage of American households touched by crime declined from 30 percent in 1981 to 23.7 percent in 1991, and the number of incidents of murder, robbery and assault has declined in almost all the nation's large cities,[13] the prison-building roller coaster continues to build steam. "At this rate," says Washington state governor Mike Lowry, "everyone in Washington State will be working in—or in—prison by 2056." [14]Washington's prison population has climbed 79 percent over the past decade.

And all this despite near-universal agreement among criminal justice experts that incarceration has little effect on crime, and may in fact make things worse by "hardening" prisoners, turning petty thieves into violent felons. "Ironic" is too mild a word to describe a political system that can't imagine spending a few hundred dollars a year extra to teach a young student how to read, that believes college tuition assistance is far too expensive and a waste of taxpayers' money, and yet easily finds the $74,862 a year it costs to keep a prisoner in a maximum-security lock-up.

In nearly all these prisons, conditions have gotten steadily worse. Politicians looking to score easy points have cut most education and training programs formerly available to prisoners nationwide, while some states have abolished television, library privileges, access to computers and weightlifting equipment, and even coffee. The chain gang, long associated with the horrors of slavery and Southern racism, is back in Alabama and Florida. Only about nine percent of all inmates have jobs or similar productive work in prison.

The Cops Are Out of Control

Outside prison walls, the mechanisms of law enforcement have been similarly beefed up. Police departments, security agencies, the Border Patrol, county sheriffs—you name it, if it has to do with enforcing the law it has more money and more power than ever before. The nation's 19,000 law enforcement agencies have long been accused of acting like an army of occupation in low-income communities and especially communities of color. Every few years, some headline-grabbing incident will spur calls for official action and reveal the extent of the problem, but for the most part once the pressure dies so does the motivation for reform.

After the Rodney King videotape was shown repeatedly on the nightly news, for example, the Justice Department promised to investigate 15,000 unresolved cases of police brutality or use of deadly force. However, the investigation has yet to produce any concrete results or conclusion. Similarly, the Christopher Commission produced a damning report in 1992 on the systemic brutality and racist abuse meted out by Los Angeles cops, echoing the conclusions of dozens of other investigations large and small, from the 1968 Kerner Commission onward. How little has changed was made painfully obvious during the O.J. Simpson trial, as tapes featuring Detective Mark Fuhrman gave a brief look inside a police agency Fuhrman revealed as viciously racist.

Little exists in the way of national studies of the extent of the problem, but various pieces of evidence give a rough indication that police killings and incidents of severe use of force declined during the 1970s and then began to rise again in the mid-1980s, reaching epidemic proportions in some cities by the 1990s.[15] In New York, for example, 41 people were killed by police in 1991, an increase of 37 percent over just two years earlier. In Los Angeles, the city has been forced to pay steadily rising amounts to victims of police misconduct: from $553,000 in 1979 to $8 million in 1990. NAACP officials say their 2,2000 local branches receive reports of police brutality almost every day; "there's a war going on against Black people," says Walter Brooks, president of the Ossining, New York chapter.[16] Similar trends are apparent in almost all low-income urban communities, especially communities of color. One of the largest settlements paid by Los Angeles County ($999,999) was to the parents of Hong Pyo Lee, a Korean immigrant killed by sheriff's deputies in 1988.

And while complaints are rising in many cities, "no one dares guess how many incidents of police brutality go unreported or unrecorded," says Ron Daniels, director of the Center for Constitutional Rights. Very few cases result in discipline for the officers involved and the mechanisms for investigating and acting on citizen complaints are essentially worthless. Large cities like San Francisco and Chicago have a backlog of cases that runs into the hundreds or even thousands, with only a few dozen settled in any year.[17] Many victims don't bother to report what happened to them, out of either fear of retribution or a feeling that nothing will happen anyway.

There is little institutional pressure for police departments to change their ways. Settlements of successful lawsuits by victims of abuse usually come out of city or county budgets, not the coffers of law enforcement agencies. Civilian Review Boards are seldom empowered to discipline officers or even to conduct independent investigations, which means that in most cases the police investigate themselves. An in-depth review of civilian review boards that appeared in the *Minority Trendsletter* concluded that most of these bodies "are more ornamental than substantive. The bottom line is that a majority of civilian complaint review boards have little real power."

The Justice Department, which supposedly looks into violations of civil rights laws, is "largely indifferent," says a report by the American Civil Liberties Union. The ACLU report noted that the department investigates fewer than half the cases brought to its attention, and in northern California, for example, has prosecuted only two police brutality cases in twenty years.[18] The complaint process itself is so difficult and intimidating that many victims either don't file or don't follow through on complaints; when it seems like the system might be paying more attention the number of people coming forward with stories of abuse and police violence rises dramatically.[19] African Americans and Latinos also fare much worse under the complaint process than whites; a *Los Angeles Times* study of 4,000 complaints found that cases filed by people of color were much more likely to be dismissed.

"The cops are out of control," is how a CCSPA study guide sums up the issue. But for CCSPA organizers, the problem of police misconduct cannot be separated from the way social ailments have been redefined as law enforcement problems. The political question, therefore, was to come up with a method of combining the two problems in one coherent strategy.

Step by Step to a Strategy

On a cool August day in 1993, community members from five organizations across the country gathered at an Oakland union hall for what was billed as the first CTWO Strategy Session. Each one of the groups—People United for a Better Oakland (PUEBLO); Denver Action for a Better Community (ABC); Direct Action for Rights and Equality (DARE) in Providence, Rhode Island; Sacramento Communities Taking Action for Neighborhood Dignity (STAND); and Tri-County United Action (Orangeburg, South Carolina)—had been through a year-long process of popular education in a series of thirteen Issue Study Groups, or ISGs. The ISGs covered diverse topics like police brutality, alternatives to incarceration, community policing, the Border Patrol, public spending on law enforcement, and proposals for change.

Each organization developed a set of recommendations for action based on what they learned in the ISGs and what the community members felt were the most pressing concerns for their neighborhoods. These recommendations were brought to the strategy session in Oakland and hammered into a rough plan for a national campaign to link police accountability with solutions to the root causes of crime. "The ISGs were very interesting," PUEBLO member and Oakland resident Maria Leal told the *CTWO Times*. "Sometimes I think people get so scared of crime that they are willing to let the police do whatever they want. But in the ISGs we discussed ways to have both safe communities and police who respect us."[20]

Leal was one of seven PUEBLO leaders who attended the strategy session. She was joined by her counterparts from the other four grassroots organizations, about thirty leaders in all. In community organizing terminology, "leaders" are members who have made a significant personal investment of time and energy in the organization. They tend to be the more dynamic and committed members, but the basic defining characteristic is a willingness to go out and get other members of the community involved in the group.

"[In the ISGs] we went step by step to developing a strategy," explains Calpotura. "The other thing the ISGs did for us, besides producing an impressive list of recommendations for how to approach the issues, was give us the time to do the hard research and find real handles for this campaign." What finally emerged from the strategy session and subsequent meetings was a framework built around four basic principles: preventing crime by reallocating resources toward social needs and conflict resolution; promoting community justice and alternatives to incarceration; fostering public participation; and holding the police accountable to the community. The CCSPA calls this their "Home Run Strategy for Community Safety" (a metaphor meant to distinguish the CCSPA approach from "three strikes and you're out").

"After that strategy meeting," says Calpotura, "we had the leadership and the basic approach in place. The trick at that point was to find some concrete handles around which we could develop both a national campaign and a way for local organizations to carry the fight to their areas."

The First Fight: Asset Forfeiture

Several years prior to the CCSPA, National People's Action and other community groups in the Chicago area decided to make an issue out of the use of the Asset Forfeiture Fund. The AFF allows police to confiscate the assets—cash, homes, cars, and anything else of value—of suspected drug dealers, and use it for law enforcement.[21] From a civil liberties point of view, the AFF is highly suspect, but the NPA had a different take. They wanted the money to go back to the community.

NPA first fought AFF on the state level, eventually forcing the Illinois state government to agree to turn over part of the money seized in drug raids to community programs. A few years later, NPA, in collaboration with the Association of Community Organizations for Reform Now (ACORN), convinced the Department of Justice to make this idea part of national asset forfeiture regulations. The new regulations, passed in March 1994, allow (but don't require) local police departments to allocate fifteen percent of their asset forfeiture proceeds to community programs for crime prevention. "This gave us a real handle on the local p.d. [police department]," says Rosi Reyes, the lead organizer with People United for a Better Oakland. "It allows us to shift some money from the cops to the community, lets the police know that we are watching them and have a way to hold them accountable, and means that the money gets used for real crime prevention."

According to the CCSPA newsletter *Rap Sheet*, "An estimated $7 billion has been seized through state and federal forfeitures since Congress expanded the asset forfeitures laws as part of the 1984 crime bill."

"For the most part there is no accounting for how the money is spent, or even how much is taken in," says Mark Davis, a researcher who worked for the CCSPA in its first year. "Cops use this windfall to buy themselves everything from the latest in super-duper cop gear to a new leather couch for the chief's office."

Thus far, of the five CCSPA member groups, only PUEBLO has been successful in getting the police to agree to the fifteen percent recommendation. In Denver, Action for a Better Community staged a noisy occupation of the downtown Denver police station simply to get a meeting with police chief David Michaud, who had ignored their repeated phone calls and letters. Since 1990, $3.2 million in asset forfeiture funds has been collected by the Denver Police Department, with eighty-three percent spent on equipment and seventeen percent on training. Not a penny goes to crime prevention or social programs. This is true in nearly every city in the country where the police receive AFF funds.

The first step for community organizations is often the hardest—finding out just how much money the police take in and what they use it for. In Sacramento, for example, despite several demonstrations, an accountability session with Chief of Police Arturo Venegas, and filing a Freedom of Information request, STAND has so far not been able to get the police to release the information. In Orangeburg, South Carolina, United Action has been turning up the heat on Sheriff C.F. "Smitty" Smith, so far to no avail.

Patterns and Practices

"Asset forfeiture is a good handle," says CCSPA coordinator Francis Calpotura, "but it is definitely not the only one, and in different places the groups will get involved in different fights, depending on what works and what moves people." In Orangeburg, for example, the AFF fight takes a back seat to constant pressure by United Action to stop racist police killings and abuse. In rural South Carolina it can sometimes feel as if the civil rights movement came and went without much effect on the police. "These cops think they can do anything and get away with it," says United Action director Kamau Marcharia. One day in 1994, the United Action offices were surrounded by the Ku Klux Klan, something Marcharia believes is connected to the group's efforts to bring police misconduct to light.

Both PUEBLO and ABC have also gotten heavily involved in struggles involving proposals aimed at young people, including gang lists and curfews. In Denver, the police department was forced to remove hundreds of names from its gang list; ABC was part of a coalition of groups that argued that the list was discriminatory and violated young people's civil liberties. Ninety percent of the people on the list were Black and Latino; names were added to the list even if the individual had never been convicted of an offense. PUEBLO's youth group (Youth of Oakland United) was instrumental in stopping a proposed curfew law for young people in Oakland.

CCSPA organizers in Oakland provide research material and help formulate strategies for member organizations. At times, all member organizations decide to work together on a particular project, but the Campaign also encourages the groups to take on specific local fights under CCSPA auspices.

Another part of the CCSPA program is a documentation project aimed at showing that the "pattern and practice" of law enforcement abuse and misconduct is widespread. CCSPA staff have created a database and circulated the format to the member organizations to provide a consistent format for recording complaints.

"Patterns and practices" is a legal term used to describe a method of determining whether a particular kind of institutional behavior is systemic or isolated to particular cases. The Clinton crime package legislation passed in 1994 was not a progressive victory, but it did include a provision for using documented patterns of law enforcement misconduct to get the Justice Department to intervene in a particular agency. As *Rap Sheet* noted: "When the Attorney General has reasonable cause to believe that a violation [of individual rights] has occurred, she may obtain equitable relief through a civil action." Federal authorities can force local police departments to change policies that lead to misconduct, such as those regarding hiring practices, training, or protocols.

CCSPA members decided that a coordinated documentation project was needed to put pressure on law enforcement agencies around the country, and indeed, some organizations such as Police Watch in Los Angles have already been carefully documenting police misconduct for years.

Another handle the CCSPA is investigating has to do with human rights. In 1994, the World Council of Churches held hearings around the country on violations of human rights in the United States by racist and brutal police departments. The Council is considering going to the UN to seek redress. CCSPA organizers say that they see this not so much as a winnable fight but as a way to highlight the systemic nature of police misconduct and keep the issue in the public eye.

Finally, the CCSPA has a number of "strategy options" lined up for use as needed. These options include plans for slowing the growth of the prison system, holding the Border Patrol and INS accountable for their use of deadly force, and developing alternative sentencing programs for youth. "In fact," says Francis Calpotura, "the cops and prisons are both too strong and too dispersed for us to take on with a frontal attack. What we have to snag them in a big web by going after them on many different levels at once.

Moving Targets

If you are poor, of color, and in trouble with the law, it's a mean season in America. An explosion in get-tough laws and official policies mean that, for community groups that want to find more humane and just solutions to community safety problems, there are an unlimited number of targets. For example, many of the most punitive law enforcement measures promulgated in recent years by the "tough on crime" politicians and citizens groups have been specifically aimed at young people, most of all young men of color. Anti-loitering ordinances, curfews, gang lists, youth mug books, lowered age limits for prosecution as an adult, and dozens of other laws and policies have resulted in an unprecedented number of young men under the control of the criminal justice system.

In most cases, however, the community response to these laws or to particularly egregious examples of police brutality is either so ineffectual that it is easily ignored, or flares up and dies down over a short period of time. In other cases, long, hard campaigns to get a civilian review board or other institutional mechanisms for overseeing the police have been defeated at the ballot box—or are coopted once in place. "The experience of fighting for civilian review boards has shown us that we can't place faith in an institutional reform in the absence of real community presence and power on the issue," says Calpotura. "This is why we are looking for a number of handles so that we can engage this fight on a number of levels, without putting all our organizing eggs in one basket."

This flexibility allows the CCSPA coordinators to maximize the benefits of having a number of local groups working on the issue. The two main criteria for local CCSPA campaigns are that the fight articulate a method of moving resources from law enforcement to social program ("crime prevention" is the CCSPA's way of describing these programs) and/or that the fight revolve around police accountability. On a local level, these campaigns have been at least moderately successful, and CCSPA strategists point out that the vast majority of law enforcement policies and spending priorities are decided on the local (city or county) level.

However, the national mood or consensus on issues of crime and punishment also plays a role in determining the outcome of even local political struggles. On this level, the CCSPA has had much less of an effect, outside of one national day of demonstrations and press conferences in Washington in June 1994.

If nothing else, CCSPA members (most of whom are from the inner city) want to draw a clear distinction between what they see as socially progressive solutions to the problem of violent communities, and the regressive "lock 'em up forever" policies promoted by many community groups. "Prevention is the key," says Robbie Smith, a member of STAND. "We have got to find things for kids to do before they get in trouble. We've seen what happens when you cut back on all the programs. It's time to turn that around before it's too late and they arrest my kid—or yours."

Portions of this chapter originally appeared in *Social Policy* and *Z Magazine.*

Chapter Eight

Native Americans Struggle for Land, Liberty, and A Toxics-Free Environment

By Andrea Lewis

Three hundred years ago, Native Americans battled heroically to hold on to land they had nurtured for centuries. Today, Native activists are fighting to keep their remaining territory from being turned into America's dumping ground.

During the late 1980s and 1990s Native American activists built a grassroots resistance movement that has taken on the U.S. government and the powerful waste disposal industry, forged unprecedented inter-tribal alliances between Indian Nations, created a national indigenous environmental justice network, and built effective working coalitions with non-Indian environmental rights organizations. In the process of challenging the merchants of toxic waste, some Native activists have also challenged their own tribal governments, leading to a renewed struggle for true democracy on the reservation.

The one thing Native Americans fought for and won, through all the broken treaties, forced marches, and lost battles, was the right to have their reservations considered sovereign nations inside the borders of the United States. Sovereignty is a critical issue in Indian Country, and a key component of Native American identity. Plans to use Indian land as a dumping ground are seen by many Native activists as attempts to undermine that sovereignty.

At the end of 1988, environmental disasters such as those at Chernobyl and Love Canal, and the two-year voyage of the infamous garbage barge Pelicano, searching for a port that would accept its cargo of 14,000 tons of toxic incinerator ash, turned up the heat on the U.S. government and the waste disposal industry to deal with the country's toxic waste problem. "The long voyage of the Pelicano is a stark symbol of the environmental exploitation of poor countries by the rich," said *Time's* January 2, 1989 cover story, "Endangered Earth: Planet of the Year." The practice of simply shifting "potentially hazardous waste from one place to another," said *Time*, "only underscores the enormity of what has become an urgent global dilemma: how to reduce the gargantuan waste by-products of civilization without endangering human health or damaging the environment."[1]

Rather than risking another Pelicano debacle, the waste disposal industry turned to the only sovereign nations living *within* America's borders for a solution to the waste-disposal problem. By the late 1980s, giant waste disposal companies such as Bechtel and Waste-Tech followed in the footsteps of smaller entrepreneurs who had approached Indian nations with proposals for waste facilities. The Chickaloon Village in Alaska was one of the first to receive such an offer. Their tribal membership rejected a Waste-Tech proposed hazardous waste incinerator in 1988. Other proposals were soon to follow.

Looking to Indian Country

In early 1990, Connecticut-based O&G Industries began negotiating with the Tribal Council of the Lakota Sioux Indians at the Pine Ridge reservation in South Dakota to develop a 5,000-acre waste dump for garbage, solid waste, incinerator ash, and sewage sludge ash from all over the country. It wasn't the first time the Pine Ridge reservation had been approached with proposals for dumps. In 1986, two entrepreneurs who held rights to 6,000 acres of reservation land proposed a disposal site for sewage sludge ash and asbestos, but regulatory discussions with the Environmental Protection Agency (EPA) stalled the plan. Over the following three years, other companies including Bechtel had separate discussions with the tribe, but none of the initial plans for waste facilities were developed enough to receive serious consideration.

The O&G proposal, floated by Amcor, a subsidiary of O&G, was a comprehensive plan that, among other things, promised to bring broad and much-needed economic development to the tribe. Tribal leaders initially voted to consider the proposal and continue discussions with Amcor. But after tribal members found out about the potential health hazards posed by an unending convoy of foul-smelling toxic waste, they quickly voted to reject the tribal leaders' decision.

O&G quickly turned its attention to the nearby Rosebud Sioux reservation. RSW, Inc., another subsidiary of O&G, proposed to build the same 5,000-acre dump on Rosebud. In November 1990, RSW signed a contract with Rosebud's Lakota Sioux Tribal Council that "specifically excluded [hazardous and toxic waste] from the types of waste that may be stored, used, and/or recycled at the facility." According to Greenpeace investigators, "Both the garbage and the incinerator ash contain dangerous chemicals and toxic metals, which will contaminate land and water."

Rosebud reservation members were outraged after discovering that the agreement had been signed without their consultation. "Our people are poor, and there is a lot of economic enticement, but many of us become very angry when we heard how this is a 'said and done' deal," said Cheryl Crazy Bull, vice president of a college located on the reservation. Tribal members promptly formed the "Good Road Coalition" to fight the proposal. With the help of the Native Resource Coalition, which had worked with the Pine Ridge Lakota Indians to defeat the same proposal, the Rosebud Indians overwhelmingly rejected the plan. "This is a survival issue for us," Native organizer Emily Iron Cloud told the *Minority Trendsletter* in 1991. "These dumps have the potential to weaken our sovereignty, and we could lose our remaining land base." "How dumb do they think Indians are?" asked Good Road leader Ron Vallandra. "We have only one thing left that the government hasn't taken, and that's our land."[2]

Native lands are attractive to the waste disposal industry for several reasons. Indian reservations are not bound by U.S. state or local permit laws, environmental regulations, or health and safety requirements. Although federal environmental laws are supposedly enforced on Native lands, in the past, the EPA has admitted that enforcing EPA policy on Indian land is difficult at best. "We don't put on our boots and go traipsing around in the desert," said Roccena Lawatch, an EPA employee. She added that the San Francisco EPA office is located 600 miles from some of the Native American reservations it is supposed to monitor, which means that they might make it out for a site visit once a year.[3]

That isolation makes the land attractive to waste merchants. "Federal and corporate bureaucrats are using the old trick to go to 'Indian Country,' conveniently geographically removed from mainstream communities," said Lance Hughes of Oklahoma-based Native Americans for a Clean Environment. "The general public doesn't know anything about this move, and given the geographic and political segregation, they probably won't hear much about it." The combination of land and poverty provided a golden opportunity for the waste industry. Native Americans continue to suffer the highest unemployment and lowest standards of living of any ethnic group in the United States. "Hoping to take advantage of the devastating unemployment, pervasive poverty, and the sovereign status of Indian land, the waste disposal industry has embarked on an all-out effort to site incinerators, landfills, and similar polluting industries on Tribal land," says a 1991 Greenpeace report. "Frustrated by intense grassroots opposition and complex permitting procedures in other communities across the United States, the waste disposal industry has set its aim on what they believe to be the most vulnerable segment of society: Indian people and Indian Land."[4]

Waste company executives strenuously denied that they were looking to exploit Native communities. Most, in fact, argued that they wanted to bring economic development to these impoverished indigenous communities. "It was devastating for me to see how poor the [Indian] people are," Maurice Hoben, vice president of O&G Industries, told a reporter in the early 1990s. "I had never seen such poverty. Putting ten, twenty, thirty people to work will give them a feel of capitalism, and a hope for future opportunity where there is no hope now. That's why they have an alcohol problem, and that's why they have a drug problem." Hoben further suggested that Indians needed to change their attitudes about the land. "If they want to live the life of Mother Earth, then they have to leave the reservation, get a teepee and go out on the Great Plains and hunt buffalo," he said. "If they stay on the reservation, they're going to have to deposit waste like the rest of us."[5]

The Sovereignty Issue

According to some activists, the federally-imposed system of tribal councils has opened the door to waste merchants, casino operators, and others looking to make a profit on Native land. Grassroots organizations that fight disposal projects have invariably found themselves fighting their own elected leadership.

The Tribal Council structure was enacted in 1934 after Congress passed the Indian Reorganization Act (IRA). This act eliminated traditional tribal governments. Under the new tribal council structure, tribal members could elect their own Council, but no checks and balances were put in place to make the elected council accountable to the tribe. The Councils were only accountable to the U.S. Bureau of Indian Affairs (BIA), which operates under the auspices of the Department of the Interior. The Councils were given the authority to disburse BIA grants to each Native American nation, and also to administer any federal programs for economic development or social services. With little oversight to determine exactly how the funds and programs are handled, Tribal Councils are rife with opportunities for graft, corruption, and self-aggrandizement.

"These guys are like little kings," explains Steve Banegas, a resident on the Barona reservation in southern California. "Once they get into office they try to take all the power, and do anything to avoid losing it. They have the power to determine who gets what [on the reservation] in the way of housing, loans, water, and electricity, and when they don't like you they can cut you off." Chief Billy Tayac of the Piscataway Indian Nation says that the tribal councils that exist today are "puppet governments. If you don't adhere to their policy they can cut your funding off, they can make you unpopular. . . So what you have got to do is be totally supportive of the United States government and their policies. If you disagree with their policies, they'll replace you."[6]

"When you question authority on the reservation you put your life on the line," says Marina Ortega, an activist who successfully fought with other tribal members to stop a proposal for a giant dump on the Los Coyotes Reservation. "There are goon squads and thugs with guns. People get killed."

Even more than the environmental menace, say activists, Native Americans are very concerned about any deal that jeopardizes their self-determination. "Once people understand that these contracts undermine our sovereignty and our lives," Paiute-Shoshone activist Paul Rodarte explained, "we've been really successful in stopping [the projects], even when the Tribal Council has sold out." In a recent dramatic reversal, for example, the Kaw Tribal Council in Oklahoma was forced to renege on a signed agreement with Waste Tech, Inc. of Golden Colorado for a hazardous waste incinerator, after Kaw people organized a "Campaign for Sovereignty."

The people of Los Coyotes, near San Diego, voted to invalidate a lease agreement for a trash dump that had been signed in 1990 by tribal chairman Banning Taylor and officials at Chambers Development, a Pittsburgh-based waste-management company. Taylor later denied signing the notarized document. "My name was forged on that lease," he said, although he went on to defend the agreement. "They offered $5,000 a month just to do environmental studies. Who wouldn't accept it? We thought we were doing the reservation some good by getting some money." According to Ortega, the founder of California Indians for Cultural and Environmental Protection (CICEP), "The sovereignty issue is really what is behind these fights. The people [of Los Coyotes] were very angry that Banning Taylor waived their sovereignty for this company, and that's what really screwed him." In a victorious statement released by the Coalition for Indian Rights, the decision to rescind the lease was hailed by Gilbert Campbell, a local activist and vocal landfill opponent. "The decision reestablishes the sovereignty of native Americans and their desire to live in peace and harmony with the land."[7]

Still, even with all the enticements of big payoffs and high-paying jobs, the vast majority of tribal councils—hundreds of them—reject proposals for waste facilities.

Enter the Nukes

In 1982, Congress passed the Nuclear Waste Policy Act (NWPA), an overdue attempt to deal with the country's growing stockpiles of nuclear waste. The goal of the NWPA was two-fold: to find a large, permanent repository for nuclear waste, and to develop facilities that would deal with nuclear waste in the meantime. This short- term plan was to develop what were called Monitored Retrievable Storage (MRS) facilities.

By the late 1980s, the NWPA was proving difficult to implement. Memories of the nuclear accidents at Three Mile Island and Chernobyl were still fresh, and states fought to keep MRS and any other kind of nuclear storage facilities out of their backyards. Although Yucca Mountain in Nevada was selected as the permanent nuclear waste site in 1987, it was clear to both the federal government and the nuclear industry that a short-term approach other than developing MRS facilities would have to be found. In 1986, federal officials started giving grant money to the National Congress of American Indians to encourage participation in disposal projects. But the real strategic push came in 1990, when the nuclear power industry created the Office of Nuclear Waste Negotiator and appointed David Leroy its first head. Leroy is the former Republican lieutenant governor of Idaho, and an experienced "motivational" speaker. His plan was simple: approach Native American communities and offer them a bargain they could hardly refuse. Any community accepting a nuclear waste dump would receive money for economic development.

To sweeten the deal even more, tribes would be given substantial sums for simply considering the proposal. Leroy took his act on the road. In 1991, he spoke at the annual meeting of the National Congress of American Indians in San Francisco. Leroy's motivational speaking training was put to good use. He appealed to the participants to draw on their "Native American culture and perspective" and "timeless wisdom" to grab the chance to become the keepers of the country's nuclear waste. Quoting the famous Duwamish Chief Seattle, Leroy added, "Every part of this soil is sacred in the estimation of [Indian] people," implying that no matter where the waste ended up, it would still be on sacred ground. He promised that any tribe that agreed to consider the temporary waste storage proposal would receive $100,000 with "no strings attached."

By May 1992, the Nuclear Waste Negotiator's office had given out twenty grants of $100,000 each to tribes that agreed to consider the proposal. But by fall 1995, after a flurry of intense Native opposition and organizing, only three tribes, the Paiute-Shoshone on the Oregon-Nevada border, the Skull Valley Goshutes in Utah, and the Mescalero Apache in New Mexico were still interested. To complicate matters, in response to lobbying by the National Environmental Coalition of Native Americans (NECONA) and other groups, Congress cut further funding of the MRS program, leaving the entire program in limbo.

Welcoming Waste

Unlike most Native tribes, some such as the Mescalero Apaches have welcomed the opportunity to take cash for storing toxic and nuclear waste. As Mescalero tribal president Wendell Chino often says, "The Navajos make rugs, the Pueblos make pottery, and the Mescaleros make money." The Mescalero Apache Tribal Council (MATC) negotiated with thirty-three utility companies to construct a privately owned and operated waste dump on the Mescalero reservation in southern New Mexico. Other MATC leaders echo Chino's position. "The Mescaleros can bear this [waste storage] responsibility because of our strong traditional values that favor protection of the Earth," MATC vice president Fred Peso told a Department of Energy-sponsored conference on high-level radioactive waste. "We can serve as reliable, trustworthy, and responsible guardians of the nation's spent fuel."

Many tribal members disagree with the dumping, and with the tribe's decisionmaking process. "The Mescalero Apache people have been diabolically and deliberately excluded," said activist Rufina Marie Laws. "At the same time, the tribe is actively being obligated to agreements and contracts without the input and consensus of the people. Many tribal members are opposed to siting nuclear waste storage on our homeland, for they believe it will be a violation of our sacred land and sacred mountain, Sierra Blanca."[8]

In December 1994, a coalition of nuclear utilities reached a tentative agreement with MATC to begin construction of a temporary high-level radioactive waste dump. When the tribe initially voted on the agreement in January 1995, the vote was 490 to 362 in favor of stopping negotiations with the utilities coalition. After a well-financed media and lobbying campaign by MATC and the powerful utilities, a second vote held two months later brought a 593-372 result in favor of continuing negotiations. In mid-1995, a group called Apache Stronghold with a rapidly-expanding membership formed to fight the nuclear waste facility.

Closed By the People

Another waste company tactic is to approach individuals rather than tribal leaders, as was the case with the Torres Martinez Indians. Most of the 500 members of the Torres Martinez tribe reside on 24,000 acres in California's arid Coachella Valley, but unlike most reservation land, which is held in a federal trust, some Torres Martinez lands were awarded to individual tribal members as homesteads. In 1989, Torres Martinez tribal member Geraldine Ibanez leased 120 acres of family-owned land to Chino Corona Farms, a San Diego-based sewage company. Soon, trucks began bringing in sludge and building a mountain of about 500,000 tons of human waste. By the time the sludge started arriving, Ibanez had already moved to her husband's reservation some 50 miles away, leaving local tribal residents to endure the smell, flies, and pollution.

In this case, sovereignty worked against the interests of Indian environmentalists. The tribe had no rules that restricted Ibanez from doing what she wanted with her land. "We have an unwritten law that anybody can do with their land allotment what they will, as long as they aren't adversely affecting anyone else," tribal chairperson Mary Belardo said. And as Ibanez family supporter Kim Lawson said, "Some of us are worried that if the tribe can stop one individual from operating a business, what's to stop others from doing the same?"[9]

On the other hand, the sludge dumping *was* affecting the health of local residents. And the dumping had bypassed BIA contractual requirements, as well as the National Environmental Policy Act, which calls for an Environmental Impact Assessment at the minimum. Tribal members were split: some supported Ibanez' right to control her land, while others were concerned about the long-term environmental and health dangers posed by the mountain of waste.

Eventually the Tribal Council adopted a resolution calling for the closure of the dump. After a five-year battle that went through the EPA, the BIA, the California Regional Water Quality Control Board, the San Diego city government, and even the White House Council on Environmental Quality, the dumping was stopped. But not before tribal activists from around the state joined with groups such as the Indigenous Environmental Network, Greenpeace, California Rural Legal Assistance Foundation, and the United Farm Workers to block the dump. For two weeks, the coalition blockaded the facility, on which they hung a sign announcing that the facility was "CLOSED BY THE PEOPLE." Finally, on October 31, 1994, a federal court issued an injunction and temporary restraining order against further dumping.

In July 1995, the five lower Colorado River Indian tribes, the Colorado River Native Nations Alliance, signed a joint resolution declaring their opposition to a proposed radioactive dump at Ward Valley, California. Proponents of the dump have spent millions of dollars on public relations campaigns, and giant corporations such as Pacific Gas and Electric have lobbied strongly in favor of the dump because it will provide an inexpensive way to get rid of wastes generated at power plant sites. The valley is a pristine part of the Mojave desert area and contains an unparalleled range of desert ecosystems. The opposition includes an impressive alliance of activist groups and the Ward Valley Coalition, which includes California Communities Against Toxics, Fort Mojave Indian Tribe, Physicians for Social Responsibility, Bay Area Nuclear Waste Coalition, and Greenpeace.

Making Connections

The battle to prevent Native American sovereignty from being polluted has pushed political organizing and networking in Indian country to levels not seen since the 1970s. The first "Protecting Mother

Earth: The Toxic Threat to Indian Lands" conference was held in July 1990 in Dilkon, Arizona. Activists from some thirty tribes in sixteen states gathered on a rodeo ground in 100-degree heat to talk about their shared problems with toxic waste and other pollutants on Native land. The tribes discussed ways to publicize their campaigns and form alliances with Native and non-Native environmental groups. "We want to get unity out of this conference," said Vickie McCullough, a Cherokee from Tahlequah, Oklahoma. "It doesn't make any difference what tribe we are, we're all one. The positive thing is, we're all networking." Thomas Banyacya delivered a message from Hopi elders that addressed waste contractor claims that toxic dumps, uranium mining facilities, and other similar projects will be harmless to nearby residents: "Maybe we can take some of these uranium spillings to Washington and spread it around the White House and tell them, 'Don't worry, it's not going to hurt you.'"[10]

The annual Protecting Mother Earth conferences continue to bring together Native activists from around North America. "It feels good," said Rodarte. "Things are really snowballing. We had 200 people in Dilkon from thirty tribes, and 500 people [at the second conference in Black Hills, South Dakota] from fifty-seven tribes."

To enrich networking and coordination, the Indigenous Environmental Network (IEN) was officially inaugurated after the second Protecting Mother Earth conference and Rodarte was appointed acting director. Rodarte initially planned for the network to play a key role in connecting individual struggles, which is especially important given that the same company will often approach several different reservations with the same proposal. Waste Tech, for example, has admitted that it wants to site fifteen incinerators or dumps on Native American land, while an internal memo from Bechtel Corporation leaked to activists suggested locating hazardous waste facilities on reservations all over the country.

Another goal of the network is to bridge the gap between the hazardous waste experts and the grassroots. "We have been successful because we are Indian people working with other Indians," Rodarte commented, "but sometimes tying into the environmental groups is like getting hooked into another bureaucracy." He explained that if Native Americans are organized, they can access the information and expertise of national environmental organizations and develop strategies on their own. Greenpeace has emerged as one of Native activists' strongest allies in the fight against toxics, but the group has also been criticized for coming on too strong and trying to run things, a charge Greenpeace takes seriously. Although Greenpeace financed the first Protecting Mother Earth Conference, San Francisco representative Bradley Angel says, "We're not here to tell people what to do, but just to provide information."

No Quick Fix

Although Native activists have built a strong resistance movement and network of grassroots organizations in their battle over toxics, they are still faced with a staggering array of social and economic problems. Many observers see the recent influx of gambling casinos and toxic waste proposals as economic quick fixes to long-term government-created problems of Native American communities. "The badly-needed services, such as hospitals, roads, schools, and jobs the DOE promises to provide for having an MRS are services that are supposed to be given Indian tribes in accordance with treaties and agreements between Indian tribes and the U.S. government," says Lila Bird, a Pueblo activist working with the Water Information Network in Albuquerque and with the National Environmental Coalition of Native Americans. Tom Goldtooth, national coordinator of the IEN, agrees. "What we want is to get the government to recognize the statutory responsibilities it has to develop tribal structures on the environment. Right now the government isn't fulfilling its obligations and if it doesn't, there's nothing else to call it but environmental racism."

While new proposals for toxic dumps in Indian Country have slowed to a trickle as a result of organized resistance by Native Americans, the fight to protect the land continues. "Some tribes that are rich in natural resources have faced unsustainable and devastating development—the removal of trees and extraction of minerals—oil, gas, and uranium mining, many of which leave contaminated tailings. Issues like safe drinking water, recycling and pollution prevention—these haven't really been priorities in the past," says Goldtooth.

Besides stemming the flow of toxics into Indian Country, perhaps the greatest success of Native activists is building an improved communications network. "IEN was conceived from the need for people to have basic support in the area of communication—bringing information to isolated communities. There is light at the end of the tunnel, as long as we continue to empower grassroots communities who have had limited ability to be informed at the local level," says Goldtooth. "But it isn't just about tribal responsibility and government responsibility. We can't let corporations and industry off the hook. As indigenous people, we feel that the corporate sector has completely exploited the sacredness of our land. We along with our non-Native neighbors are realizing the need to respond to long-term questions about toxic contamination and basic environmental protections."

Special research assistance provided by Bradley Angel of San Francisco Greenpeace. This chapter is based in part on "Protecting Mother Earth: Native Americans Organize to Stop the Merchants of Hazardous Waste," *The Minority Trendsletter*, Vol. 4, Number 4, Fall 1991. *The Minority Trendsletter* was the precursor magazine to *Third Force*. It ceased publication in 1992.

Chapter Nine

Having the Tools at Hand

Building Successful Multicultural Social Justice Organizations

By John Anner

The long-awaited age of the true international city is fully upon us, although not quite in the cheerful Disney World format expected by the advocates of multiculturalism. Urban America has become a staggeringly diverse melange of cultures and languages; it's no longer hyperbole to talk about the "global village," not with millions of the global villagers themselves living just down the street.

The changing demographic composition of many areas of the country is coupled with other shifts in the global political economy that are having severe negative effects on both urban and rural America. In brief, the unrestrained ability of international corporations to shift production and jobs just about anywhere in the world has meant disrupted communities, declining wages, and lower standards of living for most Americans—and increasing social decay and conflict.

Social justice organizations and movements have to contend with new constituents and new conditions. They have to figure out how to mobilize and organize people who may share geographic proximity and hard times but little else, in a political climate that has shifted the blame for worsening economic conditions onto the immigrants, the poor, and the powerless. And they have to figure out how to develop effective strategies for defending their constituents in an era in which progressive government-financed social legislation is close to politically impossible.

On the whole, the traditional defenders of low-income and working-class Americans have done a very poor job of building a sophisticated multicultural response to the changes outlined above, which is one reason things are so terrible. Unions, long the main bulwark against attacks on people's livelihoods, are barely awakening from a long period of political sleep. Progressive academics, professionals, leaders of national civil rights organizations, advocates, lobbyists, and politicians appear to be helpless, timid, and out of ideas, endlessly fighting symbolic battles. And for whatever reason, there is no credible leftist political party in America.

It's more or less an article of faith among progressive political thinkers that we need a new mass-based struggle for social justice featuring leadership from people of color and a diverse membership.[1] I believe the stories told in the preceding chapters show, in fact, that there is an emerging "second generation" of grassroots community and labor organizations that have developed over the past five to ten years. In the best examples, the energy and mutual respect characteristic of the politics of identity have been used to revitalize and strengthen class-based organizing and to build strong relations between communities normally divided by race, language, and culture.

No Mystery to Multiculturalism

There is no mystery to building effective multicultural social justice organizations, say many activists and organizers. A variety of organizations provide training and consultations, and, as this chapter indicates, there are specific methods available to activists and organizers. "What matters most of all," says diversity trainer Guadalupe Guajardo, of Technical Assistance for Community Services (TACS) in Portland, Oregon, "is being able to listen and learn, and having the tools at hand to make changes."

This chapter focuses on the specific tactics and strategies that social justice organizers use to build multicultural organizations, drawing on the lessons of previous chapters. Organizers can begin to confront the larger economic and political forces devastating low- and middle-income communities by building social justice organizations that can adapt to rapid changes in the demographic and cultural environment. While these organizations may not lead a national social justice movement, if and when it develops, they will train its political leaders, provide models of effective organizing methods, educate and develop memberships, keep people involved on a regular basis in community work, and test the local power structure for weak points.

A movement can draw on this base and use it to inspire large numbers of people to take action. This phenomenon occurred in California's anti-Proposition 187 movement. Established community, student, labor, civil rights, professional, and other groups sounded the alarm and laid the groundwork, but in the end a movement exploded outside the boundaries these organizations created. Indeed, one of the biggest protest marches, which took place in Los Angeles, occurred despite attempts by some "Stop 187" organizations to prevent it. A movement, when one develops, pulls in political, community, and labor organizations, but also inspires large numbers of previously uninvolved people.

At the same time, the efficacy and longevity of a movement rests on the foundation created through the daily back-breaking work of local grassroots organizing. This work must include constant attention to developing multicultural memberships and alliances.

The models and mechanisms being used to build successful multicultural social justice organizations include:

- Building personal relationships between members from different backgrounds.
- Actively engaging in solidarity campaigns, actions, and activities with social justice organizations in other communities.
- Challenging bigoted statements and attitudes when they arise.
- Holding regular discussions, forums, "educationals," and workshops to enhance people's understandings of other communities and individuals.
- Working to change the culture of the organization so that members see themselves as "members of the community"

first instead of members of a particular part of the community.

- Developing issues, tactics, and campaigns that are relevant to different communities and that reveal fundamental areas of common interest.
- Conducting anti-racism training to get people to confront and deal with their biases.
- Examining and changing the organization's practices in order to hire, promote, and develop people of color.
- Confronting white privilege and nationalism.
- Hiring, recruiting, and training more people of color for leadership positions.

It Doesn't Just Happen

Elsa Barboza is an organizer with South Los Angeles-based Action for Grassroots Empowerment and Neighborhood Development Alternatives (AGENDA). AGENDA has generally focused on the African-American community, and most of the staff and organizers are African-American. In 1994, says Barboza, "we decided to move towards organizing in the Latino community for the simple reason that we have a lot of new immigrants from Central America in the neighborhoods. We wanted to [make AGENDA] an authentic multicultural organization, but we learned an important lesson: it doesn't just happen."

AGENDA organizers quickly found that bringing monolingual Spanish-speaking members to the general membership and committee meetings was not effective in involving the new Latino members. AGENDA staff decided instead to form a separate organization known as the Latino Organizing Committee. The plan is to build leadership in the Committee, take on a few organizing campaigns around issues of particular concern to those members, and "agitate and educate" the South Los Angeles Latino community. "In the beginning we used the same strategies and tactics for everyone," says Barboza, but it simply didn't work in terms of attracting more Latinos to the group.

One solution is to define issues and campaigns so as to make them relevant to all members of the organization. For example, People United for a Better Oakland (PUEBLO) conducted a campaign in 1994 to force Highland Hospital to hire more professional translators. At first glance, this would not seem to be an issue of major concern to the native English speakers in the group. However, PUEBLO organizers and leaders successfully argued that nobody can get adequate medical care if some doctors and nurses are being called away from their duties in order to translate for a patient who doesn't speak English.

AGENDA has taken a different tack, working instead to research and develop campaigns that are of particular concern to the Spanish-speaking members. At some point in the future, when the Latino Organizing Committee has had enough experience organizing, the two organizations will be merged. In the meantime, AGENDA is conducting what they call "educationals" with all their African-American members to "demystify" the changing demographics of Los Angeles, and show how low-income communities of color face similar challenges and problems.

In terms of specific mechanisms to overcome prejudice-based resistance on the part of current members, "we don't have any 'diversity training' going on just yet," says Barboza, "but we'll probably need it in the future." She says that people get past any initial resistance pretty quickly, however, and see through to the larger self-interest that unites people of color. All the members come together for general membership meetings and selected planning meetings. Translation is conducted by an interpreter who sits with the Spanish-speaking members.

As we saw in Chapter Two, another community group that started out all African-American and gradually changed as the demographics of the neighborhood changed is Direct Action for Rights and Equality (DARE) in Providence, Rhode Island. DARE is a powerful ten-year-old organization well known at City Hall; part of that power, say staff members, comes from the group's representative membership. In the beginning however, the few Latino and Asian members seldom participated in DARE's activities. Looking back, says former organizer Libero Della Piana, three things stand out as "holding back" other members: language, culture, and the issues DARE worked on.

In contrast to AGENDA, DARE set out from the beginning to avoid creating two different organizations. "We did have a Comité Latino where meetings are conducted only in Spanish," says Della Piana, "but we didn't want it to become a separate group because we didn't think we'd be able to later turn it into a cohesive organization."

Della Piana says that organizers who want to build multicultural organizations have to ask themselves if they are making everyone feel welcome and wanted. Translating all written materials is critical, he says, because it not only makes all members feel part of the organization but is a way of visibly showing that the group is serious about being multiracial. At this point, Providence is changing again, experiencing a big influx of immigrants from South Asia, and DARE "desperately needs" an organizer who speaks one or more of the languages of the Indian subcontinent.

In the Heat of the Struggle

Perhaps the most common way that multicultural groups deal with diversity in their memberships is through a political ideology that emphasizes how the struggle at hand transcends differences of race, age, gender, or sexuality. The Committee Against Anti-Asian Violence (CAAAV) is a New York-based community group that has been active and visible on issue ranging from hate crimes to police brutality and economic exploitation. The group's 2,500 members are diverse, but all Asian. "We are a pan-Asian organization," says staff organizer Saleem Osman, "so in our group there is no hostility, only solidarity, because we are all working together for the same things." Although it is certainly true that there is a good deal of mutual dislike and often active hostility among the large variety of immigrant communities that have found themselves living side by side in urban America, it does seem to be the case that these differences can be set aside in the heat of the struggle.

An additional factor might be that the members of multicultural groups tend to be self-selecting. If someone is really not happy being part of a diverse membership organization, they tend to simply not join in the first place, or leave as the group changes. Finally, differences that seemed of intense importance in the region of origin (Chinese versus Japanese, Salvadoran versus Honduran, North Indian versus South Indian) start to lose their meaning once the reality of life in the United States sinks in and the different groups find that more unites them than separates them.

On the other hand, says Osman, working in coalition with other groups requires a lot of internal education. "Our members, who are taxi drivers, garment workers, and vendors mostly, need to be challenged to look at [their prejudices]." Prejudice against Latinos and African Americans among CAAAV members was clearly revealed during city council hearings on a bill that would have granted taxi drivers the right to refuse to pick up any individual based on their appearance. CAAAV organizers knew that drivers were supportive of the bill because it gave them the right to refuse rides to African-American men.

"We had to do a lot of work with the members on that one," says Osman. "That was a law aimed directly at African-Americans. So we said 'no, we won't support it because it's racist.' But first we put together a video and used it to educate the drivers" in day-long training sessions.

CAAAV then took the issue one step further, appearing at public hearings to argue against the law, sometimes surprising African-American civil rights groups. "The best way to overcome prejudices between [communities of color]," says Osman, "is to work together in solidarity with each other to build unity." For this reason, says Osman, CAAAV has actively sought to build a working relationship with Puerto Rican and African-American groups active in the fight against police brutality.

Organizations such as CAAAV, AGENDA, and PUEBLO frequently are called upon by other local groups to attend public hearings or demonstrations or turn out their members for community events. Wendall Chin, an organizer for a multiracial group called San Francisco Anglers for Environmental Rights (SAFER) says that an important way to overcome racial prejudices is to get the members involved in soliciting secondary support from other groups and in joining those groups' actions. SAFER is an environmental justice organization sponsored by Communities for a Better Environment that organizes low-income anglers who fish in the San Francisco Bay for food as opposed to sport. SAFER has joined forces with Texas-based Fuerza Unida in their campaign against the Levi Strauss Company, which is headquartered in San Francisco. Similarly, they have been actively involved with PUEBLO and Asian Immigrant Women Advocates (AIWA), both of which are located in Oakland, not too far from SAFER's main area of operations.

The relationship between external and internal politics is not always as easy and obvious as staff and leaders would like; this is especially true when the senior staff is white. "One of the reasons we had such trouble with the NTC [National Toxics Coalition]," says Sonia Peña, "is that the people in charge figured that because they were part of the struggle and did good political work they therefore could not be considered racist or sexist or authoritarian or any of those things and didn't have to deal with the issues when they came up in the organization." Peña was on the NTC board at the time of its demise due to intractable internal problems in 1993; she is the lead organizer for the multiracial community group Denver Action for a Better Community.

The anti-AIDS activist group ACT UP and the gay visibility network Queer Nation also started to come apart at the seams in the mid-1990s, in part because of their inability to cope with demands by members of color that the particular needs of their communities receive greater attention. Similarly, at the 1995 National People's Action (NPA) conference in Washington, D.C., a group of Latino delegates stormed the stage and took over the microphone from executive director Gale Cinotta. Led by Juan Mireles, they demanded that the NPA start translating meetings and conference plenaries into Spanish and that a minimum of 25 percent of the delegates to the next year's convention be Latino. Mireles told freelance writer Daniel Cordes that part of the problem is that the NPA—as a predominantly white and African-American organization—doesn't see the need to organize around issues of particular concern to Latinos or to figure out mechanisms to bring in a more diverse membership.

For both NPA and NTC, shared concerns among the membership about declining neighborhoods, redlining, and economic justice were not enough to paper over conflicts among staff and/or members of different races. Some formal mechanism is needed for "surfacing" these conflicts, letting them come out into the open, and resolving them as a group.

This can be as simple as not letting bigoted comments pass without comment. When prejudices are aired openly in a meeting or other event, say organizers, it can poison relations unless it is dealt with openly. "I remember one time at a meeting where we had whites, Blacks, and three or four Mexican members," says SAFER organizer Wendell Chin, "and an outspoken white leader commented that she was glad that [the anti-immigrant California ballot initiative] Proposition 187 had passed because of the problems too many immigrants were causing. I looked over at the Mexican [members] and they weren't saying anything. So I had to step in and intervene."

"It's always better if the challenge comes from inside the membership of the group," says PUEBLO organizer Danny HoSang, "because then the members who are being challenged don't feel like they are being singled out by the staff. But if nobody speaks up, the staff organizer has to do it. It's not only about consciousness-raising. All the members of the group need to feel like they are welcome and valued."

Sometimes a more involved process is required. When tensions surfaced between Asian and Black participants in a year-long program called A New Collaboration for Hands-On Relationships (ANCHOR), program director Rinku Sen decided to skip the actual program for that week and hold a series of discussions about the differences between the two communities. "Just because we call ourselves people of color doesn't mean we have the same backgrounds," says Sen. "Someone who was born in Cambodia and moved into a Black neighborhood in Oakland might experience racism as a daily fact of life. But that experience itself might be different than it would be for a Black person, and of course it is filtered through their history and current expectations."

Speaking My Language

Multicultural organizations are usually multilingual. PUEBLO, DARE, and other community groups have invested in a number of simultaneous translating machines. "They are a costly but highly effective tool," says PUEBLO lead organizer Rosi Reyes. The machines allow members to be seated anywhere in the room, instead of being segregated in one area, while the translator speaks quietly into a transmitter worn over the head. Receivers are smaller than a pack of cigarettes, with tiny earphones.

Some groups break meetings into segments, with some parts translated and others held in one language. Monica Russo, an organizer with a Florida local of the UNITE, uses this technique with a membership that speaks English, Creole, and Spanish. Day-long trainings, for example, feature monolingual sessions combined with collective meals and informal periods.

Most organizers warn, however, that translation demands more than simply literally transcribing what is being said. In order to transmit the real meaning and invite participation, says Peter Cervantes-Gautschi, director of the Portland, Oregon Workers Organizing Committee, "the critical thing is that the [translator] has to be into the movement. Because if [that person] doesn't really understand what we're trying to accomplish, then they are not going to get it right."

From White to Rainbow

"There are two main obstacles to building multiracial social justice movements," says Libero Della Piana, who edits *Race File* at the Applied Research Center, "nationalism and white racism." Although many barriers divide people of color from each other, diversifying white organizations presents a different and more difficult set of challenges. "People of color generally understand racism as institutional," says Guadalupe Guajardo, "while to white people white privilege is virtually invisible, and they see prejudice as being something personal.

"Sometimes the hardest thing is to get people to face the reality that racism does exist even though polite people don't make racist comments anymore. But the only way to reach people and get them to examine how they benefit [from white privilege] is to start from the assumption that people are basically good. If you call folks racist, you will just make them defensive and won't get anywhere."

When working with an all-white group that wants to become multicultural, TACS trainers lay out five concrete areas to examine and consider changing: 1) the recruitment process, including where it is done and what the qualification requirements are; 2) planning, i.e., who is at the table when plans are being made; 3) decisionmaking, i.e., who is involved when decisions are made, both in formal and informal settings; 4) resource allocation, including money, access, and power; 5) promotion and leadership. Promoting people of color to leadership positions is vital, but only if these individuals have a base of support, are going to be given power and resources, and are held accountable.

"People need solutions," says Guajardo. "We help them find a new model based on an alliance-building or partnership idea, instead of seeing diversity as a win/lose kind of thing."

A number of other organizations around the country conduct similar trainings, ranging from "racial awareness training" to "diversity management," "prejudice reduction," and "coalition building."

Changing the Mix

A criticism frequently directed at national community organizing networks is that the staff organizers and directors are mostly white, while the people they organize are predominantly people of color. This is certainly true for NPA, the Association of Community Organizations for Reform Now (ACORN), and to a lesser extent the Industrial Areas Foundation (IAF). The same criticism is leveled at labor organizations and the progressive press. There are more people of color working at the average metropolitan daily newspaper than at all the left-wing magazines in the country combined.

This situation—at least on the community organizing side of things—is responsible for at least three significant trends in grassroots social justice organizing that appeared in the 1980s and developed throughout the 1990s. First is the rapid growth of independent organizations in communities of color not connected to any of the community organizing networks or unions, including many of the groups described in this book.

Second is the formation of organizer training programs specifically designed to train organizers of color to work in community and labor organizations comprised of people of color. Of these, by far the most prominent is the Center for Third World Organizing (CTWO), which has trained several hundred organizers of color through ten years of programs such as the Minority Activist Apprenticeship Program (MAAP) and the Community Partnership Program. Along with the organizer training programs, CTWO has also developed a model of community organizing that relies on organizers of color.

Finally, many emerging social justice organizations have made an explicit commitment to leadership diversity. The New Party constitution, for example, states that 50 percent or more of the leaders of local chapters must be people of color and 50 percent must be women. Greater diversity in the organizing staff can bring immediate rewards for community and labor organizations; it is now pretty much accepted by labor leaders that white men are the least effective organizers.[2]

Teamsters Local 175 in Seattle, Washington wanted to organize Asian women working in private postal facilities. The notion that these women could not be organized, says organizer Michael Laslett, was partly due to the fact that nobody had ever tried, and partly due to the expected barriers of culture, race, and language. He brought on two Asian-American interns from the AFL-CIO Organizing Institute to go into one particular shop, which resulted in a victorious union drive. "Having Asian organizers is what made organizing this company possible," he said.

In 1994, the United Electrical Workers (UE) were able to organize Mexican workers at a SteelTech factory in Milwaukee by importing an organizer from a sister union in Mexico. Labor organizers of color can be pretty scarce. A perhaps apocryphal story has it that the Oil, Chemical, and Atomic Workers Union at one time employed the only Vietnamese labor organizer in the country, and used to lend him out to other unions that needed a Vietnamese-speaking organizer.

Fluid Identities

The strategies for diversifying that work with this generation may not work with the next one, however. According to Libero Della Piana, when push comes to shove, the color of the organizer matters less than the person's commitment, especially when working with youth. "Of course it helps to have a diverse organizing staff," he comments, "but in the end that's not what it's about. Members respect the staff that's willing to do the work. It's a delicate balance."

In fact, say some youth organizers, most of what has been outlined above is based on strict definitions that don't fit with the mixed identities and intensely multicultural lives of urban youth. These young people don't need to be taught how to get along with other cultures, nor do they necessarily identify with the racial categories that guide the previous generation.

"It's pretty wild," says Next Generation co-director Mike Perez, who used to work at the Oakland-based youth program Encampment for Citizenship. "Race and class intersect in different ways for young people than they do for their parents." Many young people believe they can choose their racial identity based on how they feel. "I didn't have enough attitude to be a Black girl," one white high school student told *YO!* editor Nell Bernstein, explaining why she dressed like a *cholita*, or Latina gansta girl.

"You have white kids coming in saying they are just as much a 'nigga' as any Black kid since they come from the same 'hood," says Perez. "You have Asian kids dressing hip-hop and talking [African-American dialect]. Other Black kids talk and act 'white,' in the eyes of their friends. Identities are very fluid, but it's what being young is about now."

Della Piana agrees: "During the campaign to stop Prop 187, the main organizations active in Oakland tried to define it as a Latino issue. The high school and junior high students who organized and marched in the streets refused to see it that way. Their notion of what the fight was about was based on who was in and who was out.

"Kids base their identity on the basis of a complicated formula of territory, race, class, and aspirations," he continues. "There's a connection between kids that nobody understands; they can relate to each other [across racial boundaries] in some way adults have a hard time with."

It is probably true, as some youth organizers argue, that the intense problems that race, gender, and sexuality caused for older political groups and movements will not be as much in evidence as younger people start to move into leadership positions in social justice organizations. Perhaps "the fire next time" will burn brightly in rainbow patterns. But if we want social justice organizing to move beyond the limitations of identity struggles into an enlightened next phase, with justice, community, democracy, and true solidarity on the top of the agenda, we would do well to remember what Elsa Barboza said: It doesn't just happen.

Portions of this chapter originally appeared in *The Neighborhood Works.*

Contributors

John Anner

John Anner is founding editor and publisher of *Third Force* magazine, and publications director of the Center for Third World Organizing. A frequent contributor to magazines such as Z, the *Progressive, Native Peoples, Social Policy*, and *Crossroads*, Anner directs the Community Journalism Cross Training program, and is a veteran activist in student, community, and solidarity organizing.

David Bacon

David Bacon is a California writer and photographer. His work documents the changing demographics of workers and unions in the Southwest, and concentrates on issues of labor, immigration, and international politics. He worked in a semiconductor factory in Silicon Valley for many years, and was a labor organizer for two decades with the United Farm Workers, the United Electrical Workers, the International Ladies Garment Workers, and other unions. He is an associate editor of Pacific News Service and a member of the Impact Visuals photographers' cooperative.

Gary Delgado

Gary Delgado has been part of the teams that founded the Center for Third World Organizing, ACORN, and the organization he currently directs, the Applied Research Center. He has published numerous articles on community and labor organizing, focusing on the role of race and ethnicity in shaping social change initiatives. He lives in Oakland with his wife Marcia, his son Kenan, and his daugher Chela.

Van Jones

Van Jones graduated from Yale Law School in 1993. He is now director of the police misconduct project at the San Francisco Lawyers' Committee for Civil Rights.

Hoon Lee

Hoon Lee participated in the first KIWA summer activist training.

N'Tanya Lee

N'Tanya Lee is a coordinator of PACE's Lesbian/Gay People of Color Curriculum Project.

Andrea Lewis

Andrea Lewis is a San-Francisco-based writer, editor, and musician. She has previously woked on the editorial staffs of *Mother Jones* magazine, HarperCollins Publishers, and is currently the Senior Editor for *Third Force* magazine. Her writing has appeared in *The Black Women's Health Book, The Womenspirit Sourcebook,* and in a variety of periodicals, including *The San Francisco Examiner* and *Out/Look* magazine.

Clarence Lusane

Clarence Lusane has worked for nearly twenty years in national Black politics. He is most recently the author of *African Americans at the Crossroads: The Restructuring of Black Leadership and the 1992 Elections.*

Lisa North

Lisa North is a lesbian mother and elementary school teacher. North is also a member of PACE.

Don Murphy

Don Murphy, a public school teacher and member of PACE, is active in the Black community and education struggles in New York City.

Mark Toney

Former DARE director Mark Toney is currently the director of Strategic Tools, Inc., a consulting organization specializing in grass-roots organizing.

Juliet Ucelli

Juliet Ucelli is a public school social worker and a member of PACE.

Notes

Notes to Introduction

1. Delgado, Gary. *Beyond the Politics of Place*. Oakland: Applied Research Center, 1995.

2. Quoted in Sitkoff, Harvard. *The Struggle for Black Equality*. New York: The Noonday Press, 1993.

3. Wei, William, *The Asian American Movement*. Philadelphia: Temple University Press, 1993.

Notes to Chapter One

1. Not to be confused with the front for the Los Angeles Police Department known as Drug Abuse Resistance Education or D.A.R.E.

2. Meaning independent organizations of workers, often immigrants, that fight for the rights of the membership without forming a union. Examples include Asian Immigrant Workers Advocates in Oakland, California and Black Workers for Justice in Rocky Mount, North Carolina.

3. A target in organizing terms is the person who can give you what you want, the one with the power to make a decision in your favor.

4. "Activists Representing Immigrants Protest Conditions at Almacs Store," *Providence Journal–Bulletin*, July 4, 1992.

5. *Retail Food Inspection Report*, Division of Food Protection and Sanitation, Rhode Island Department of Health, July 3, 1992.

6. "Almacs Agrees to DARE's Demands," *The Providence American*, August 1, 1992.

7. David Paulhus, Almacs Public Relations Director, Correspondence to DARE, August 25, 1992.

Notes to Chapter Two

1. Of a total enrollment of 995,000 students, 590,000 were eligible for the free lunch program and 421,000 came from families collecting public assistance. Figures on the New York public schools from the Population Studies Unit of the Department of Education.

2. Four out of the top six countries of origin for immigrant students are countries with predominantly Black populations: the Dominican Republic, Jamaica, Guyana, and Haiti.

3. See Jonathon Kozol's book *Savage Inequalities* for a harrowing trip through the worst of the public schools, including some New York City schools, and a description of how "magnet schools" can actually work to worsen conditions for the majority of students.

Notes to Chapter Three

1. See for example Yoon, In-Jin. "The Growth of Korean Immigrant Entrepeneurship in Chicago," *Ethnic and Racial Studies*, 18:2, April 1995.

2. "Shared ethnicity created avenues for exploitation," argues Dong Ok Lee in his study of how immigrant communities "commodify ethnicity" as a way to make it despite handicaps of culture and language. Lee, Dong Ok. "Commodification of Ethnicity," *Urban Affairs Quarterly*, 28:2, December 1992.

3. It must be pointed out, however, that the prevailing image of the Korean community's position in American society remains one of "Asian entrepeneurs versus the Black/Latino underclass." See for example Umemot, Karen. "Blacks and Koreans in Los Angeles," in *Blacks, Latinos and Asians in Urban America*, edited by James Jennings. Wesport, Conn.: Praeger, 1994.

Notes to Chapter Four

1. See Peters, Cynthia. "Progressive Activism in the United States," in *Haiti, Dangerous Crossroads*. Boston: South End Press, 1995.

2. See Jean-Pierre, Jean. "The Tenth Department," in *Dangerous Crossroads*.

3. See Loeb, Paul Rogat. *Generation at the Crossroads: Apathy and Action on the American Campus*. Loeb puts the academic year 1989-1990 as a watershed, marking the dividing line between a quiet 1980s and a much more active 1990s.

4. Such as SNCC leader and momentary Black Panther Stokely Carmichael's quip that the best postion for women in the movement was "prone."

5. For example, convincing the school cafeteria to purchase locally-produced food, setting up a recyling program, or connecting the campus to community-based struggles to limit toxic dumping.

6. See Alexander, Nicolas. "What Ever Happened to the Free South Africa Movement?" *Third Force*, March/April 1993.

7. Chomsky, Noam. "Democracy Enhancement: Part II, the Case of Haiti," *Z Magazine*, 7:7, July 1994.

Notes to Chapter Five

1. "Garment Shop Owner Disappears," *Oakland Tribune*, July 7, 1991, and "Garment Owner Surrenders to Face Fraud Charges," *Oakland Tribune*, March 17, 1992.

2. "Unpaid Seamstresses Look to S.F. Designer," *San Francisco Examiner*, October 5, 1992.

3. Interview with author, March 1994.

4. "The Textile Industry is Looking Threadbare," *Business Week*, September 16, 1991.

5. "Dades New Fit in Clothing," *Miami Herald*, March 5, 1990.

6. "Labor and Lace," *Los Angeles Times* Magazine, August 1, 1993.

7. "U.S. Apparel Industry Finds Edge," *Christian Science Monitor*, October 17, 1989.

8. Delgado, Gary. "Campaign Notes," May 1983, Center for Third World Organizing.

9. Lipsky, Michael. "Protest as a Political Resource," *American Political Science Review*, 62, December 1968.

10. Interview with author, April 1994.

11. This is the same Helen Kim who participated in the KIWA training described in Chapter Three.

12. Interview with author, March 1994.

13. In late 1995 the ILGWU merged with the Amalgamated Clothing and Textile Workers Union (ACTWU) to form a much larger garment workers union named UNITE.

14. Interview with author, April 1994.

15. Interview with author, April 1994.

16. McClintock Inc. was successful in blocking an endorsement in the corporation's home city, San Francisco.

17. Interview with author, April 1994.

18. See "Protest as a Political Resource," op. cit.

19. "Old Union Tactics?" *Los Angeles Times* Magazine, August 29, 1993.

20. Letter from Jessica McClintock Inc. to AIWA supporter Leon Somoplinsky, March 12, 1993.

21. "Garment Workers Fight for Back Pay," *San Francisco Examiner,* February 16, 1994.

22. "New Contract Expected to Stabilize Bay Area Garment Industry," September 14, 1993 News Release, Office of Information, U.S. Department of Labor, San Francisco Wage and Hour Division.

23. Interview with author, April 1994.

24. "U.S. Crackdown on Garment Makers," *San Francisco Chronicle,* January 11, 1993.

25. Foo, Laura Jo. "Response to KCBS Editorial on Jessica McClintock," December 28, 1993, Asian Law Caucus.

26. "Chinese Garment Workers Resist Fraud Charge," *Union Wage: A Working Women's Newspaper,* November/December 1981.

27. "Two Points of View," Op-Ed pieces by Helen Kim and Jessica McClintock, *Korea Times,* December 15, 1993.

28. "Faith in Ordinary People," *Daily Bruin,* February 9, 1994.

Notes to Chapter Six

1. As just one example, immigrants from El Salvador rebelled in Washington, D.C. following a police shooting in 1991.

2. Except where otherwise noted, all quotations are from interviews with the author.

3. Garcia, Michelle. " Latino Students Blow Out of School," *Third Force,* Volume 3 #1. March/April 1995.

4. Johnston-Hernandez, Beatrice. "Women Fight Free Trade," *Third Force,* Volume 2, #2. May/June 1994.

Notes to Chapter Seven

1. For a historical analysis of what has been called at different times the "lumpenproletariat," "the dangerous classes," and currently "the underclass," see Jones, Jacqueline. *The Dispossesed: America's Underclass From the Civil War to the Present.* New York: Basic Books, 1992.

2. Resistance "may be expressed spontaneously through crime, increased aggressiveness and revolt rather than in a conscious or organized form but it still tends to endanger the social order and becomes objectively political." Melossi, Dario and Massimo Pavarini. *The Prison and the Factory.* New Jersey: Barnes and Noble, 1981. Translated from the Italian by Glynis

Cousin. Original edition published in 1977. I'm not arguing here that all crime represents a protest against the social order, only that crime as an indicator of social decay—and the response to it—eventually takes on a political dimension.

3. Piven, Frances Fox and Richard Cloward. *Regulating the Poor: The Functions of Public Welfare.* New York: Vintage Books, 1993 (second edition).

4. Lusane, Clarence. "A Radical Approach to the Drug Crisis," *Third Force,* 2:6, January/February 1995.

5. Lee, Henry. "Drug Money Comes Back to Oakland," *San Francisco Chronicle,* April 5, 1995.

6. Interview with the author, December 1994.

7. Nick Alexander has found that in some cases police-sponsored Neighborhood Watch groups that have raised the issue of police abuse have been shut down by the police, while residents who are concerned about police violence generally stop attending meetings after it becomes clear that the issue of police conduct or policing style is not on the agenda. See Alexander, Nick. "Taming the Paramilitary Monster," *Third Force,* September/October 1993.

8. Mauer, Marc. *Americans Behind Bars: The International Use of Incarceration 1992-1993.* Sentencing Project, 1994.

9. Hallinan, Joe. "Blacks Surpass 50% of U.S. Prison Population," *San Francisco Examiner,* January 20, 1995.

10. Weinstein, Corey. "Fighting the American Gulag," *Third Force,* January/February 1995.

11. U.S. Dept. Of Commerce, *Statistical Abstract of the United States, 13.* Mauer, op. cit.

12. Anderson, David. *New York Times* Magazine, June 12, 1994.

13. Kruas, Clifford. "Urban Crimes Rates Falling This Year," Reported in the *New York Times,* November 8, 1994.

14. Quoted in Smolowe, Jill. "...And Throw Away the Key," *Time,* February 7, 1994.

15. Harrison, Eric. "Brutality: A Hard Issue for Police," *Los Angeles Times,* April 4, 1991.

16. Tobar, Hector. "Police Abuse of Blacks on Rise, Say Leaders of NAACP Units," *Los Angeles Times,* July 10, 1990.

17. See Rodriquez, Antonio H. "So, You Have a Complaint?" *Los Angeles Times,* March 14, 1991, and Watson, Carol. "Complaints Meet a Wall of Silence," *Los Angeles Times,* March 10, 1991.

18. Rosenfield, Seth. "Beating Cases Brushed Aside, Lawyers Claim," *San Francisco Examiner,* April 16, 1991.

19. Matthews, Jay. "Brutality Reports Soar Following L.A. Beating," *Washington Post,* March 26, 1991.

20. *CTWO Times,* Fall 1994.

21. The assets are first turned over to the Justice Department, which then kicks back a percentage to the local police departments.

Notes to Chapter Eight

1. Langone, John. *Time,* January 2, 1989.

2. Anner, John. "Protecting Mother Earth: Native Americans Organize to Stop the Merchants of Hazardous Waste," *Minority Trendsletter*, Vol. 4, Number 4, Fall 1991.

3. Lambrecht, Bill. "Indian Tribes Lured By Money From Toxic Waste Incinerators," *St. Louis Post-Dispatch,* June 25, 1990.

4. Angel, Bradley. "The Toxic Threat to Indian Lands: A Greenpeace Report," June 1991.

5. Lambrecht, Bill. "Sioux Fight Plan For Dump," St. *Louis Post-Dispatch,* December 16, 1990.

6. Thomas, Lois. "Native Democracy," *Third Force,* Volume 3, #5. November/December 1995.

7. Wallace, Amy. "Indians Have Change of Heart Over Dump," *Los Angeles Times,* July 8, 1990.

8. Hanson, Randel D. "Indian Burial Grounds for Nuclear Waste," *Multinational Monitor,* September 1995.

9. Russell, Dick. "Moving Mountains," *Amicus Journal,* Winter 1995.

10. Sitts, Richard. "Dilkon Environmental Meet Stresses Unity," *Independent: The Truth Well Told,* June 30, 1990.

Notes to Chapter Nine

1. Manning Marable, for example, argues that "the new black liberation of the twenty-first century must look outward, embracing those people of color and oppressed people of divergent ethnic backgrounds who share our ethnic vision." "Building Coalitions of People of Color: Beyond Racial Identity Politics," in James Jennings, ed. *Blacks, Latinos and Asians in Urban America: Status and Prospects for Activism.*

2. In terms of winning contracts. AFL-CIO studies show that white male organizers won contracts at a lower rate than either women or people of color.

Index

A

B

C

D

E

F

G

H

I

J

K

L

M

N

O

P

Q

R

S

T

U

V

W

Y

Z

About South End Press

South End Press is a nonprofit, collectively-run book publisher with over 200 titles in print. Since our founding in 1977, we have tried to meet the needs of readers who are exploring, or are already committed to, the politics of radical social change.

Our goal is to publish books that encourage critical thinking and constructive action on the key political, cultural, social, economic, and ecological issues shaping life in the United States and in the world. In this way, we hope to give expression to a wide diversity of democratic social movements and to provide an alternative to the products of corporate publishing.

Through the Institute for Social and Cultural Change, South End Press works with other political media projects—Z *Magazine;* Speak Out!, a speakers bureau; and the Publishers Support Project—to expand access to information and critical analysis. If you would like a free catalog of South End Press books or information about our membership program, which offers two free books and a 40 percent discount on all titles, please write to us at: South End Press, 116 Saint Botolph Street, Boston, MA 02115.

Visit South End Press, Z Magazine, Z Media Institute, Left On-Line University, and the Chomsky Archive on Z Net at http://www.lbbs.org

Other Titles Of Interest

The Last Generation: Poetry and Prose
by Cherrié Moraga

Food for Our Grandmothers: Writings by Arab American and Arab Canadian Feminists
By Joanna Kadi

About the Author

John Anner is founding editor and publisher of *Third Force* magazine. He is a frequent contributor to *Z*, *The Progressive*, *Native Peoples*, *Social Policy*, and *Crossroads*.